THE PERFECT
PUPPY

THE PERFECT
PUPPY

GWEN BAILEY

THE READER'S DIGEST ASSOCIATION, INC.
Pleasantville, New York/Montreal

For John Rogerson for patiently teaching me until I too, could bridge the gap between dogs and their owners. GB

First printing in paperback 2007

A Reader's Digest Book
Edited and designed by
Hamlyn

Reader's Digest and the Pegasus logo are registered trademarks of
The Reader's Digest Association, Inc.

Executive Art Editor: Vivienne Brar
Commissioning Editor: Samantha Ward-Dutton
Photographer: Rosie Hyde
Designers: Jessica Caws and Keith Martin
Copy Editor: Sylvia Sullivan
Production: Juliette Butler

First published in Great Britain in 1995

ISBN-10: 0-7621-0863-0 (paperback)
ISBN-13: 978-0-7621-0863-3 (paperback)
ISBN-10: 0-89577-839-4 (hardcover)

Address any comments about *The Perfect Puppy* to:
The Reader's Digest Association, Inc.
Adult Trade Publishing
Reader's Digest Road
Pleasantville, NY 10570-7000

For more Reader's Digest products and
information, visit our website:
www.rd.com (in the United States)
www.readersdigest.ca (in Canada)

Printed in China

7 9 10 8 (hardcover)
1 3 5 7 9 10 8 6 4 2 (paperback)

CONTENTS

PREFACE

Life for young puppies should be one long, happy adventure. Too often, it is a confusing time when people expect too much of them and they get into trouble for breaking rules they did not know existed.

Dogs in real life are, unfortunately, not like Lassie or Rin-Tin-Tin. They do not automatically understand our every word and thought. They are a different species, with different capabilities and communication systems. They need our gentle assistance to guide them toward a better understanding of our ways and to help them learn what we want from them. Puppies, like children, need our love and protection. They need to be controlled just enough to make them nice to live with, but not so much that their spirit is stifled.

For some years I have worked with dogs that do not make it through the whole of their lives with the same owner. This is often because the first owners did not put enough effort into acquiring the knowledge needed to bring up a puppy correctly. As the dog behavior counselor for the Blue Cross (one of the largest animal welfare charities in the United Kingdom finding homes for unwanted dogs) I have seen plenty of relationships between dog and owner that were crumbling or had broken down completely. If the partnership cannot be repaired, the loser is always the dog.

Two years ago I began to run puppy socialization classes in the hope that I could get to the source of the trouble between some dogs and their owners before it developed into a major problem. It was then that I realized how easy it is to put people on the right track while the puppy is young enough to change its behavior quickly and the owners are still enthusiastic enough to learn. On the whole, owners are not irresponsible or uncaring, but they often lack the necessary know-how to do the job properly. It would take several dog lifetimes to get it right by trial and error, but it becomes much easier if we all learn from each other's mistakes and successes.

This book is a result of what I have learned from my work as a dog behavior counselor, running puppy classes, and seeing those dogs that I helped educate develop into well-behaved, happy adults. Feedback from the puppy owners attending my classes taught me what worked and what did not. I have learned a lot, both from the "problem" dogs I have helped and from the puppies in the classes. I hope that, by writing this book, I can pass on some of this knowledge and help dog owners whom I could otherwise never reach.

At first glance, the amount of effort needed to rear a puppy correctly may seem daunting. However, this book is designed to help you bring up your puppy with a minimum of error, and it covers all aspects thoroughly. It is unlikely that you will have to radically alter your natural ability to raise an infant, but this book will give you the extra knowledge needed to do the job well.

Planning in advance and getting things right the first time is quicker, in the long run, than having to sort out problems later on. To make the best use of this book, put the ideas and suggestions into place *before* things begin to go wrong. In this way, you will be able to avoid the problems that so many owners run into. This will make life easier, and better, for you and your puppy.

This is a book about how to influence your puppy's behavior and how to mold his future character only. You will also need to find out how to care for your puppy's physical needs. Many books are available that specialize in this subject

I refer to a puppy as "he" rather than "she," although there is no reason for this other than to save writing he/she or "it" throughout. There is no difference between the worth of male and female dogs; both have qualities that can make them rewarding lifelong companions.

Acknowledgments

My grateful thanks go to John Rogerson. Without his help, encouragement, and inspired insight into the canine mind, this book would not have been possible. Most of the ideas and techniques given here are his, and I am indebted to him for willingly sharing his expertise with me. Thanks are also due to other pioneers in the field — in particular, Ian Dunbar (who introduced me to puppy classes), John Fisher, Terry Ryan, and Peter Neville.

A special thank you is also due to Tony Orchard for his original thoughts on kind methods of training, and I am very grateful to him and his wife, Jenni, for organizing the puppies to be photographed from their puppy classes. I am indebted to the puppy owners who gave up their time willingly and loaned their puppies for the photo shoots, and would like to thank Rosie Hyde for taking such wonderful photographs in difficult circumstances.

A number of people read and commented on the first draft: John Rogerson, John Fisher, Tony Orchard, Julie Sellors, Andrew Edney and Brian Kentish. This improved the manuscript considerably, and I am grateful for their enthusiasm for the idea and encouragement during the early stages of writing. A special thank you goes to Sam Ward-Dutton of Reed Illustrated Books for believing in the book from the outset and for steering it through all the necessary stages so expertly and with such good humor.

Thanks are also due to the Blue Cross. They believed in me sufficiently to allow me to become the first dog behavior counselor to work for an animal welfare charity and, hence, to allow me to help many more dogs than I would have been able to otherwise. A special mention should also be given to my colleague Tina Kew, whose support, encouragement, and undying faith that I would eventually learn enough to become competent helped me through those early difficult days when I was struggling to learn.

Finally, I would like to thank Len for putting up with me during the years it took to learn everything about the subject, and my dogs Winnie, Beau, and Sam, from whom I learned so much and whose repeated visits to the attic room where I was writing provided much-needed company and meant that this book was finished ahead of schedule.

Gwen Bailey

Publisher's acknowledgments

Reed Illustrated Books would like to thank the following organizations and people for lending their dogs and for modeling:
Tony and Jenny Orchard and Loki and Quilly; Pamela Allison and James; Mrs. Hargreaves and Rosie; Hazel Williamson and Heidi; Mrs. Turner and Jenna; Mrs. Brookes and Jazz; Helen Goldstein and Scrubbs and Lucy; Carolyn Rathbone and Millie; Sally Stephens and Merlin; Joanne Adams and Bryn; Dr. Anne Edwards and Ethel; Pauline Hosker and her family of Anatolians; The Guide Dogs for the Blind Association; Margot Osbourne and Anne Bore and the Puppy Socialization Class of Hazelmere and District Dog Training Club; Rachel Hurst and Wayne Blackwell and Poppy; Mandy Jenkins and Charlie; Keith and Andrea Jarrett and Meg; Ms. Fountain and Monty; Wendy Smith and Biggles; Karen, Sharon, and Kevin Mekepeace and Millie; Sammy and Beau (the author's dogs); Mrs. Diana Cromwell and Chelsea; Mrs. Anne Shepherd and Clipper and Glen; Miss Sue McLean and Ollie; Philip Shepherd and Mopsy; Stephen, Sara, and Francis Vipond and Mars and Pippa; Ms. Kate Coleridge and Lupo; Mr. Woolley and Floss; Penny Cooper and Dixie; Martin and Julia Richards and Sultan; Thomas and William Howe; Scruffy Goodspeed; Carla Niewenhuizen and Bella; Mrs. Darkins and Tilly; Mrs. Joan Schweir and Bryn; Mr. Locke and Lottie; Joanne Davis and Bobbie.

Chapter One

THE RAW MATERIAL

You may think that, inside, one puppy is much like another. But in fact, by the time he gets to his new home, each puppy will react differently to the world he encounters. Each will have a different outlook on life based on his unique genetic makeup and the experiences he has already had. For this reason, starting off with the right puppy will make the job of raising him easier. This chapter is designed to help you choose. If you have acquired a puppy already, this chapter will help you to understand how his background will influence his future behavior.

Genes — A Blueprint for Behavior

Whether your puppy has a pedigree with a noble ancestry or is a cross-breed of mixed parentage, the genetic material that has been handed down to him will have a bearing on how his character develops.

Our present-day breeds of dog were developed years ago. Dogs that were not suited for specific tasks, such as hunting, were selected and paired. A dog with excellent vision and a dog with the chasing instinct would combine to make an excellent hunting dog. Each breed was created by selecting for particular traits, generation after generation, until each member of that particular breed has a predisposition toward a set of inherent behaviors typical of that breed.

If, for example, your puppy comes from a long-established line of Dachshunds, a breed originally developed to unearth badgers, he will be more prone to digging than, say, a Deerhound, which was bred to hunt deer. A Collie will be more likely to chase than a Cocker Spaniel. Dobermanns are more likely to be domineering than Dalmatians.

Inherited predispositions form the raw material that you will be working with, and in order to make the best of your particular puppy, it is helpful to know exactly what you are dealing with. You can get information like this from books about your chosen breed. You will then begin to build up a picture of what your puppy has been bred for and his likely characteristics. If you do this before you acquire your puppy, you will be able to tell if his qualities are the ones that you want in your pet dog; if not, try to find a breed more suitable for your family and lifestyle.

Characteristics of 12 popular breeds

Breed	Originally bred for	Amount of socialization needed	Strength of will	Activity level
Labrador	Retrieving fish	Average	Medium	Medium
German Shepherd Dog	Herding and guarding	Lots	Strong	Medium
Border Collie/Working Sheep Dog	Herding sheep	Lots	Medium	V. high
Jack Russell Terrier	Killing rats and foxes	Average	Strong	High
Yorkshire Terrier	Killing rats	Average	Weak	Medium
West Highland White Terrier	Killing rats and foxes	Average	Strong	High
Golden Retriever	Retrieving game	Average	Average	Low
Cavalier King Charles Spaniel	Companion	Average	Weak	Low
Cocker Spaniel	Flushing game	Average	Strong	High
English Springer Spaniel	Flushing game	Average	Average	V. high
Boxer	Hunting bear and boar	Average	Average	High
Staffordshire Bull Terrier	Fighting other dogs	Average	Strong	Medium

Finding out about inherited predispositions is harder if you have a puppy of unknown parentage. If your puppy is a first cross from two pedigreed dogs, it is fairly likely that he will inherit a mixture of the two sets of characteristics — it is unlikely that you will know his ancestry, or you may know the mother but not the father. In this case it's wise to acquire a general knowledge of the various traits that different breeds can have and to watch for their appearance in your own puppy. (See the table above for a summary of characteristics of 12 popular breeds.)

Many people choose a dog simply because they like the way it looks rather than considering how it is likely to behave. This is not the best basis on which to choose a companion that will probably be living with you and your family for possibly the next 15 years or longer. You may be lucky enough to choose the right one, but to strengthen the odds, it is better to consider very carefully your own circumstances — what you want from the dog, how much time and energy you have, what your own characteristics are — and then decide which breed of dog is best suited to you and your family.

If you know only one or two dogs of the breed you have selected (or perhaps none at all), try to find other people who own a dog of that breed and talk to them about their dog's characteristics. Dog owners are

11

No two puppies in a litter are ever the same, even though they come from the same parents.

usually only too pleased to talk about their pets. Ask them about the animal's bad points, as well as the good, because many owners and breeders overlook defects in their enthusiasm to point out the virtues of the breed.

Finding the puppy with the genetic makeup that suits you and your family best will make it more likely that you will succeed in raising a well-adjusted pet. A good companion is much easier to create if you start with the most suitable genetic material. It is therefore worth giving this part of the equation considerable thought beforehand.

If you have already acquired your puppy and realized that you may not have chosen wisely, do not despair. It is possible to turn a puppy that does not have the most suitable genetic makeup into an ideal adult dog. You may just have to work a little harder and accumulate greater knowledge in order to do so.

Whatever breed you choose, your dog's temperament as an adult will depend not only on his genetic makeup but also on the way he is raised. Although his breeding is important, by far the biggest influence on his character will be environmental — i.e., the way in which you bring him up and train him. Getting this part right will ensure that even a puppy whose parents have not been carefully selected for temperament becomes a perfect pet.

Regardless of their breeding, all puppies are different. No two in a litter are the same, and puppies with the same ancestry are not identical. Once you know what traits your particular breed of dog is likely to have, you can watch for them as your puppy develops, and shape and use them to your advantage or control them as you wish. Most of this book is devoted to ways in which to do this.

Working Strain or Show Stock?

During the early development of the breeds, dogs were selected for how they acted rather than for how they looked. Times have changed, however, and now most pet dogs come from show stock, which means that the predominant requirement is to produce a dog that is typical of the breed in appearance.

Since only physical appearance is tested in the show ring, only the more caring breeders are concerned about the temperament of individuals in their particular breeding line, or take steps to ensure that only dogs with sound character are used for breeding. Even then, the temptation to use a stud dog with excellent conformation but a less-than-perfect temperament that will be likely to produce champions in the show ring, may be too much for some breeders.

Some dogs are still bred for their working ability. Sheepdogs are a prime example. The best puppies from each litter will be kept to be trained and worked. The surplus will find their way into pet homes. Before you take on a dog with this sort of background, consider whether you want a dog that is capable of running 20 to 30 miles a day and has the stamina to keep going all day every day. Kept in an ordinary home, where the owners have their own busy lives to think about, working dogs such as these can drive their humans mad, unless they become demented themselves in the process.

If a breeder proudly shows you photographs of the parents at the final of a sheepdog trial, winning an award for the Best Police Dog of the Year, or competing in the Iditarod sled-dog race across Alaska, you would be wise to consider carefully whether you want a pet dog with these inherited abilities.

Dogs are usually bred for their beauty, their working ability, as pets, or simply by accident. It is only by finding out as much as you can about the various forms of ancestry available can you make an informed choice as to which line of breeding will be right for you.

Where your puppy comes from

Where your puppy comes from is important. As we shall see in Chapter 6, the process of socialization should already be under way by the time puppies are ready to leave their mother. How thoroughly this process has been carried out will make quite a difference to how your puppy eventually turns out.

The best possible start for a puppy is to be born into a busy and lively household where he can experience all the many sights and sounds that he should become familiar with. If he is handled (carefully) by children and adults every day, played with by visitors, and has met other friendly dogs, by the time he gets to you he will be well on the way to being well-balanced and confident in all situations. If, on top of all of this, the litter was planned and care was taken to use parents with sound, friendly temperaments, then you have the best possible recipe for future success with your dog.

Puppies from some other sources can turn out just as well, providing you are careful in your choice. Caring breeders who keep their dogs in kennels but who take time to bring them into the house and socialize them are a good source, as are some rescue centers that keep their puppies in a place where they get plenty of human contact and different experiences from an early age.

Some puppies, because of their genetic makeup, need less socialization than puppies of other other breeds. But buying a puppy that you know has had plenty of pleasant experiences in a varied environment will get you off on the right foot.

Beware of buying a puppy from places where little care has been taken — for example, a farm where the puppies are kept outside and have never been taken into the home, a show kennel where no effort has been made to handle or socialize the pups, a pet shop where there is no way of knowing how the puppies have been raised, or a puppy-farm outlet where large numbers of puppies of different breeds are brought together just to offer the customer a wide choice.

Puppy-farmed dogs, bred *en masse* in unsuitable conditions specifically for the pet trade, are well known for having temperament and physical disorders. It is unlikely that care will have been taken to select the parents; often any dog that looks vaguely like the breed required will do, and the early stress and trauma of being born in such circumstances and then transported long distances at a very early age take their toll. Some very peculiar behavior problems and temperament disturbances have been seen in dogs bred in this way.

To make sure you are not buying such a puppy, insist on seeing the puppy with its mother, and be very suspicious if the breeder makes excuses as to why this is not possible. Go back for another visit if necessary. Never accept a puppy that the breeder or supplier offers to deliver to your home or meet you halfway "to save you a long trip." Beware of advertisements that offer puppies of several breeds.

Seeing the mother with the puppies gives you a good indication of your puppy's future temperament. Nervous traits are usually inherited, and puppies that experience their mother's fear and aggression toward strangers at an early stage are likely to learn this behavior and show it in later life as they mature. I have often seen people who have a nervous aggression problem with their dogs, and when I ask them if they saw their dog's mother, they say: "Oh yes, but you couldn't get anywhere near her." One couple, whose dog was extremely aggressive toward strangers and who had bought the puppy knowing that both its parents were guard dogs, commented that they wanted their dog to be a guard too, but not to bite people!

Lastly, beware of the unscrupulous breeder or dealer. I know of one man who breeds German Shepherd dogs that have very unreliable temperaments and sells them with the assurance that he will take them back should they not prove suitable for any reason. He usually gets them back again when they are about one year old because the owners are unable to handle them; then he sells them for a second time as guard dogs.

You can tell a lot about your puppy by watching how he behaves in the litter and by meeting his mother.

When to Take Your Puppy Home

Opinions vary as to the best age for a puppy to leave its mother and littermates. The advantages of its staying in the litter have to be weighed against the advantages of its being with the new family.

The longer the puppy stays with the mother and its littermates, the more it will learn about canine communication and the better it will cope with encounters with other dogs later in life. Puppies that leave the litter too soon, such as orphaned puppies that need to be hand-reared,

About six weeks old is the best age to take your puppy home. After this age its time is better spent learning to be with a human family rather than living in the litter.

will miss out on play with other puppies. They may be unable to deal appropriately or adequately with encounters with other dogs, which may lead to aggression problems when they mature. Not only do they fail to read signals that other dogs are sending them, but they often give out entirely inappropriate ones themselves, which in many cases provokes aggression from other dogs. They also miss out on the discipline that the bitch instills in her puppies from a very early age. This will make it a lot more difficult for the new owner to gain respect when the puppy eventually goes to its new home.

However, the longer a puppy stays in the litter, the less chance it has to learn human ways. If a puppy stays in a litter too long, as in the case of puppies that are "run-on" by breeders until about six months of age to see if they develop well enough for show purposes, they may be less competent in encounters with humans, making them less than ideal as pets. Such dogs often enjoy the company of other dogs more than human companionship, are often difficult to communicate and play with, and may be shy and more prone to showing nervous aggression toward strangers.

So the decision of when to take a puppy home has to be a compromise. Since it is more important for pet dogs to be able to interact well with people rather than other dogs, this should be given more weight. Current thinking is that a puppy about six weeks of age is old enough to have learned a lot about life in the litter, and that time after this is better spent learning to be part of a human family. Do not take a puppy older than eight weeks unless you know for certain that it has already been well socialized with humans and has had many varied experiences and plenty of individual attention.

CHAPTER TWO

A PUPPY'S-EYE VIEW OF THE WORLD

Ancestors of our domestic dogs, the wolves, evolved long ago to be co-operative hunters of large prey. Their brains and bodies developed to serve this purpose and to allow them to detect, chase, and kill large prey by cooperating and coexisting with each other in packs.

These abilities, motivations, and behaviors have been handed down, to some degree, to our domestic dogs. Consequently, our dogs have very different needs and abilities from humans. Before you can bring up a puppy successfully, you have to be able to look at things from a dog's point of view. This means being aware that it often has a different picture of the world from what we might expect.

A puppy sees the world from a perspective that is very different from our own.

Exposing the teeth (left) means different things to humans and dogs.

Motivations for dogs' actions may be different from our own because other things are important to them. This may lead to misinterpretations on both sides as we look at things from our own point of view only. Humans' actions, such as smiling and staring, can be misunderstood. Showing the teeth in humans is a sign of friendship, whereas in a dog pack it is an obvious signal that the pack member has the capability to bite and is likely to do so if the provocation continues.

Hierarchy is crucial to the survival of a wolf pack, and our own pet dogs are often much more conscious of their status within their human family than we realize (see Chapter 8).

As well as having different motivations and interests from ours, a dog's view of the world is different from our own. In order to understand puppies, it is important to know about these differences.

The submissive "grin" exhibited by some dogs when greeting humans may resemble a snarl. Although such a "grin" is a sign of appeasement, it is often misinterpreted as aggression, especially by visitors who are unfamiliar with the dog.

Body Language and the Spoken Word

Dogs usually communicate with each other by using body language. This involves posturing with tail, ears, body positions, eye contact, and facial expression. A great deal of information can be passed between two dogs in this way, and body language is their substitute for the spoken language that we humans rely on.

In the wild, dogs have little use for vocalization, and so they find our words relatively difficult to learn. This explains why they learn hand signals more readily than spoken commands.

Since dogs have such a different language system from ours, difficulties of communication frequently occur between the two species when

A happy, confident puppy with ears forward, nose lowered, and tail upright, exploring his environment.

Wrestling games enable puppies to practice dominant and submissive postures.

Head up, ears back, and tail wagging, this puppy shows excitement while his littermate remains neutral.

Valuable lessons can be learned about other puppies in the litter while fighting for possession of a toy.

The winner lies down with his trophy and places one paw on it to show the others who it belongs to.

21

they interact. Dogs often misinterpret human intentions, and humans often misread their dogs, which leads to all sorts of problems.

To overcome this, you will need to learn to read your puppy's body language and carefully teach him to respond to each spoken command you want to use. You can also improve communication with your puppy by substituting very obvious body postures and signals for words.

Crouching down and sending open body signals will make him feel welcome.

Puppies understand many of these without training because some things do translate well from their own language. For example, crouching down and sending "open" body signals is an obvious welcome signal. Towering above your puppy with a stiffened posture, staring eyes, and tight mouth will signal a threat.

Your puppy will watch you more than you expect, and will read your body signals rather than listen to you. He quickly learns to interpret your mood and knows what you are feeling, without your saying anything.

Towering over your puppy and staring at him may make him feel threatened.

Eye Contact

Dogs often use direct eye contact to threaten each other. An adult dog may caution a misbehaving puppy by staring at it. A high-ranking, or dominant, dog will make piercing eye contact to indicate to a subordinate dog that it is breaking a rule. People sometimes do this with a glare, but most often eye contact between people and their dogs is friendly, with eyes wide open and no thought of discipline.

Puppies being brought up in a human family need to learn the difference between the two types of eye contact. They need to know that another dog staring at them across the park may mean business, whereas a new human friend who is staring at them is being friendly. This should happen quite naturally during the socialization process, although some shy puppies may need extra help to learn this.

If staring intimidates your puppy, let him get used to it by occasionally catching his eye and talking to him in a friendly manner. If your puppy is shy and looks away from you, continue to talk to him in the same voice until he looks back at you. When he does, reward him with a game or praise him. You will gradually be able to reduce the puppy's anxiety while increasing the time he is willing to gaze back up at you.

A well-socialized puppy stares comfortably into his owner's eyes.

Dogs Live in a World of Scent

Sight is our primary sense, and we learn most about our world with our eyes. In dogs, however, the sense of smell is far more important, and much of the information they gather from their environment goes in through their nose. Watch a dog and owner as they enter a new room. The human will use his eyes to find out what goes on there, whereas the dog will go sniffing around to discover what he needs to know.

Dogs can detect odors in a way that we find hard to contemplate. They can easily follow the route taken by a person who passed through a room hours, sometimes days, earlier, leaving no visible signs, or they can sniff out minute amounts of drugs or explosives through layers of packaging and containers.

A dog's sense of smell is known to be at least 100 times keener than our own and may be even greater. The area inside the dog's nose that detects scent is about 14 times larger than ours, and the part of its brain that processes the information is proportionately larger and better developed. Consequently, dogs are not only better able to detect smells than we are, but they are more interested in them too.

A great deal of information can be gathered with just one sniff.

In the wild, the sense of smell would have been of great value to dogs, not only for the detection of prey, but for the maintenance of social groups and the defense of territory. Being able to tell who your friends and enemies are, when they all look similar, is very useful. Knowing the sex, state of health, age, and reproductive state from one sniff can answer a lot of questions!

This amazing ability has been handed down to our own pet dogs, and it helps to explain why they are so fascinated by scents, and why they go to great lengths to gather information through their nose. By sniffing every lamp-post or putting their noses into all the wrong places when investigating new people, dogs are gaining information about their environment that may be useful to them later, in much the same way as you or I will obtain clues about our environment by using our eyes.

Eyesight is Less Well-Developed

To a dog, a white ball on green grass stands out much more than a red one.

In comparison with our human ability to see, a dog's sense of sight is less well developed. Its vision is not as detailed as ours, and it recognizes objects by shape and form rather than by detail and texture.

Dogs are not color-blind, but they see color less well than humans. It is more difficult for them to distinguish between certain colors; for example, a red ball on green grass will blend in, whereas a white one will stand out.

Dogs can see better at night and in dim conditions than we can, because they have a reflective layer at the back of their eyes that traps any light entering and allows them to make more use of it. This is why they can run off at top speed into the darkness on winter walks without crashing into trees and fences (and why their eyes "shine" when caught in the beam of a car's headlights).

Dogs are also much more sensitive to movement than we are, especially when it occurs at ground level. We are able to see stationary and moving objects equally well, whereas dogs are much more likely to see objects that are moving and ignore stationary ones. This means that they can detect the slightest movement of our bodies and allows them to anticipate our actions before we have deliberately moved.

25

Hearing is Acute

Dogs with pricked ears can orient them more easily, which enables them to pinpoint the source of a sound. This is more difficult for dogs with large hanging ear flaps, which can be only slightly raised.

Dogs are more sensitive to sound than we are. Sounds that can barely be heard by us at a given distance can be detected by dogs that are four times as far away. So there is no need to shout!

Dogs can also hear a higher range of frequencies, which means they hear sounds in the ultrasonic range that we cannot detect. In the wild, this enables them to locate small prey, such as rodents, which communicate in squeaks of a very high frequency. This ability explains why dogs can respond to "silent" dog whistles while we hear nothing.

Some breeds of dog, such as Collies — which have been bred to hear a shepherd a long distance away — have more sensitive hearing than others. This explains why they develop phobias about thunder and gunfire so easily. If such noises sound loud to us, imagine what they must sound like to a puppy.

CHAPTER THREE

THE NEW FAMILY

The household that a puppy grows up in will have a significant impact on his future character. Whoever lives in the household — whether they be old or young, aggressive or timid, happy or miserable — will leave an impression on him. Whether the people in the house have previously owned dogs, or if there are children, dogs, or other pets in the family will also have an influence.

Reflections of Ourselves

If you look at a group of six-month-old puppies and their owners, it is relatively easy to tell which puppy belongs to which owner. This is because puppies tend to reflect directly their owners' characters as they mature, possibly because they share the same emotional experiences. Happy, loving people, for example, tend to have happy, outgoing puppies, whereas miserable, boring people tend to have puppies that are quiet and disinterested.

People who live alone with just their Poodle for company, tend to have shy, introverted Poodles. A boisterous, happy, lively family with a Rottweiler tends to have a dog that would not hurt a fly but will push you over in his enthusiasm to lick you. A family with tensions and conflicts, whose children take their frustrations out on the dog, tends to have a mean dog that flies at you unexpectedly.

Any children in the family tend to be reflections of their parents too. If, during puppy classes, the children sit quietly, politely listening to what you have to say, the chances are their puppy will be well behaved. If the children are not well controlled by their parents and keep interrupting despite being told not to, there is a strong possibility that their puppy will be over-boisterous and willful.

I suspect that this is so because people tend to bring up their children and puppies in the same way that they were brought up themselves. The influences that shaped their characters are similar to those that will be shaping their children's and puppy's characters, and so it is likely that they will all have similar ways of behaving.

Think about how you were brought up by your parents. If you were punished a lot as a child and overcontrolled, consider what effect this will have on the puppy you are about to raise. If you were brought up in a way that made you extroverted and outgoing, how will this affect your puppy? Were your parents always shouting at you in a vain attempt to make you obey, or were they quietly in control?

Take a look at your own family and any children that you may have. Do you have the kind of temperament that you would like to see in an adult dog? How quickly do you get angry? How placid are you? Are you outgoing and lively or are you calm and introverted? If you add all of the family's characteristics to those of the breed of puppy you have chosen, it will give you a good indication of what your adult dog will be like. If your prediction of the future characteristics of your puppy are not the ones you would like to see, consider how to change the way you bring him up so that he develops differently.

Once you are aware that you have a choice about how you bring up your puppy, and that you do not have to follow the example set by your parents, it becomes much easier to decide on your training methods. Have a look at dogs belonging to other people if necessary, and see if you like their characters. If so, find out how they were brought up.

Discuss the puppy's upbringing with the rest of your family so that you are all in agreement. That way, you should set the scene for producing an adult dog with a temperament to suit you all.

Living Alone

Situations where there is only one person and one dog in the household tend to produce intense relationships. So much affection, time, and effort is expended on the relationship that other people can be excluded. This often produces a dog that is very intolerant of outsiders, particularly those coming onto their territory.

In addition to the isolation from the outside world, single owners will often give the puppy many privileges that family owners will be too busy to give. As a result, the puppy may grow up to think that he is higher in status than his owner and this, coupled with a lack of socialization, can lead to overtly aggressive protection of the owner.

If you live alone, you will need to work extra hard at socializing your puppy. You will also need to guard against allowing your puppy to grow up thinking it is more important than you and your friends, even though you may think that it is!

Children in the Family

Families with children tend to be lively and busy, which is good for socialization purposes. The negative side is that often too much is happening to allow much attention to the puppy's education; the

owners may be swept along on the tide of events, and suddenly notice one day that the puppy days are over and that they now have a boisterous, untrained adult dog to deal with.

To make sure that your puppy doesn't pick up any bad habits, supervise any play between your children and the puppy.

Sometimes parents are too busy to exercise, play with, and educate their puppy and without really considering the consequences this is often left to unsupervised children. But if left to their own devices, children, especially young ones, will often unintentionally teach a puppy bad manners.

Leave a young puppy to play unsupervised throughout its puppyhood with several young children, and you will end up with an adult dog that has learned to chase, jump up, and nip at legs or arms. Being stimulated by movement and a desire to join in children's games, this is natural behavior for a puppy.

A puppy that learns to have fun excitedly chasing children and nipping at their ankles will see no harm in doing this as an adult. Children may think this is funny while the puppy is still small, and may encourage it, but they will not think it so clever when the dog is fully grown. Worse still, other children who do not know your dog may not realize that he is intent on play when he bounds toward them. No matter how friendly your dog is being, it could scare a child enough for the authorities to believe that your dog was dangerously out of control in a public place, which could lead to prosecution.

If you have children, you will need to ensure that they teach your puppy only good behavior. Teach the children what to do when the puppy jumps up or pulls at their clothes. Teach them how to let the puppy know what they want, and how to play acceptable games. Discreetly supervising their activities will prevent either side from learning or doing the wrong thing.

Remember that toddlers are only babies themselves; they may pinch, pull, and throw things that may hurt the puppy. Puppies, with their needle-sharp teeth, can also hurt, and you will need to be there to intervene on behalf of either or both parties if necessary. Older children can tease or be intentionally cruel, just because they are at that age when they are finding out about their world. Teenagers are generally much too interested in their own lives to show more than a passing interest in the puppy and it is probably unwise to rely on them to meet the puppy's needs. However, all children are capable of showing great love and affection to a puppy and often make better playmates than adults if shown the right direction.

By giving the situation careful thought, bringing up a puppy with your children can be, and should be, a pleasure and education for them both.

Another Dog in the Household

Many owners acquire a new puppy as company for their existing dog, especially if they are away at work during the day. Unfortunately, this can lead to the puppy's relating more to the other dog in the household than it does to its owners, unless the owners take steps to prevent it.

A puppy on its own in a family without another dog will have to learn human ways, because humans are its only source of companionship. However, a puppy that has another dog in the house already has a friend that can speak the same language and play the same games. It will have no urgent need to learn the ways of humans. Unless you limit the contact your puppy has with your existing dog, he will prefer to be with him rather than with you. Problems will then inevitably arise, since you will not have as close a relationship as that between owners and a single dog. As your puppy grows up and becomes an adult, he will be less willing to do as you say, and be more difficult to control and to live with as a result. For example, when you call your dog in the park, he may not understand you because he has not learned human language and gestures very well and, because he has a stronger bond with other dogs than he does with you, he will prefer to remain with them anyway.

If you have an older dog in the family, or have two puppies from the same litter, or you regularly (i.e., nearly every day) meet another dog that your puppy plays with, you will need to take extra care. It is important to spend more time with your puppy than he spends with other dogs. He can still play with other dogs and puppies, which is important for socialization, but this time needs to be limited. Since, at first, the quality of play with you will not be as good as it is with other dogs, you should aim to spend at least three times as much playing time with your puppy as he spends with other dogs each day.

To achieve this, you will need to separate him from your other dog if they are left alone together for any length of time, either while you work during the day, or at night. It is best to have a mesh partition between them (in some cases a stairgate works well, as long as the older dog does not jump over it). This enables them to keep each other company, but they cannot play together unless you are there to supervise. It is also important that your puppy learns to be left alone completely, without the company of the other dog (see page 140).

When you want to spend time with your puppy, first confine him while you have a good game with your older dog. Then put the older dog out of the room while you give your attention to the puppy. Otherwise, your older dog will try to join in the games, the puppy will try to play with the older dog, you will get frustrated because your puppy does not want to play with you and, because you are now annoyed, your puppy will try harder to play with the other dog and keep away from you!

It is also a good idea to take your puppy out without your older dog. You can then devote more attention to him, and he will learn to be confident when out alone and not to rely on the other dog for support.

When you do allow your puppy and older dog to play together, it is important to stop their games whenever they get too rough or when your puppy becomes overexcited or bites your older dog too hard. This is because your puppy will attempt to play with dogs he meets outside in the same way as he has learned to play with your dog. Other dogs are unlikely to

If you already have a dog, it is important to make sure that your puppy does not come to prefer spending time with your dog rather than with you.

tolerate rough play, particularly as your puppy matures, and this will lead to fights. To prevent this, stop any play that other dogs, unfamiliar with your puppy, would not tolerate.

If your older dog decides to discipline your puppy by growling, snapping, or holding him down, do not interfere unless you fear for your puppy's safety. Sometimes your adult dog will need to discipline your puppy to teach it its place in the pack. By interfering, you will be altering the natural balance that will otherwise exist between them.

Keep control of all the contact your puppy has with other dogs until he has reached maturity. By ensuring that he spends more time with humans than with other dogs, you will help him to grow up as a human-oriented dog. He will be much easier to train and live with than a dog that likes other dogs best. You will have formed a strong bond between the two of you, and your dog will relate better to you and to other humans as a result.

Two From the same Litter?

People often acquire two puppies from the same litter so that they will be company for each other and play together while they are young. The bond between them, already strong because they are siblings, will be stronger than any bond they have with their owners if they are allowed continual access to each other.

In order to prevent this, you will need to find as much time for both puppies individually for play, training, and general companionship as most owners would give to one. For this reason, unless you have a great deal of time and energy, it is inadvisable to try to bring up two puppies of the same age simultaneously.

Two puppies from the same litter will have a strong bond between them, which may exclude the owners.

Other Pets

Other pets in the household help to socialize your puppy with other species and allow you a chance to teach control during exciting situations.

Introduce your puppy to any other pets you have while he is still very young. He will then accept them as other members of the family.

    If a young puppy is introduced to a pet of another species while he is still very young, he will usually accept it as just another member of the family. As an adult, a dog that was brought up with other pets is far more likely to tolerate the introduction of new pets as you acquire them.

    The instinct to chase, catch, and kill small, fast-moving animals can sometimes overcome a dog, and no dog should be trusted alone with small, easily damaged, prey species.

CHAPTER FOUR

DEVELOPMENTAL STAGES AND WHAT TO DO

All puppies follow the same pattern of development, passing through the same stages from infancy through to maturity. It is important to know these stages and to realize what responses your puppy is capable of at any particular time in his life. If you do, you will not expect too much from him or miss out on making the most of an opportunity at a critical stage in his development.

The speed at which puppies progress varies a little. Some individuals pass through certain stages quickly and others take longer than expected. Generally, puppies of smaller breeds tend to develop more rapidly, often reaching maturity before one year old, whereas puppies from larger breeds can take longer, some being 18 months before maturing fully. What follows is an average time scale that most puppies conform to.

Newborn Period: 0 to 2 Weeks

During this short phase, the puppy mostly sleeps and suckles. It can crawl and will try to find the warmth of littermates or its mother if it feels cold. It needs the mother to stimulate urination and defecation, which she does by licking the genital area. Eyes open at around 10 to 14 days, but vision is poor for the first few weeks.

Transitional Period: 2 to 3 Weeks

The teeth begin to appear. The puppy learns to walk and lap liquids. The ears open toward the

end of the third week, and the sense of smell begins to operate. The puppy develops the ability to urinate and defecate by itself.

What to do: The responsibility for what happens to puppies during this time lies with the breeder. It has been found that puppies subjected to mild stress at this time are better able to cope with other stresses later on. Picking up each puppy every day, looking at them, and perhaps weighing them constitutes mild stress, and conscientious breeders will do this. Each puppy should be picked up once a day and gently held in different positions.

Socialization Period: 3 to 12 Weeks

This is a critical period. During this time, appropriate experience with humans, other dogs, and the environment is essential if the puppy is to develop into a successful pet. This period can be divided into three stages.

First stage: weeks 3 to 5

The puppy will be in this stage when it reacts visibly to a loud sound. Bitches will begin to discipline their puppies with a growl, usually to prevent them from feeding at will.

At 3 to 4 weeks, the puppy's sight, hearing, and sense of smell are becoming more efficient. It begins to eat solid food, bark, wag its tail, and play-bite other pups. The puppy will attempt to leave the sleeping area to urinate after waking at this age.

At 4 to 5 weeks, it paws, bares teeth, growls, chases, and plays prey-killing (head-shaking) games. It begins to carry objects in its mouth. The puppy begins to learn to inhibit its bite during play with littermates.

Second stage: weeks 5 to 8

Facial and ear expressiveness are seen. Weaning begins. The puppy acquires full use of its eyes and ears and becomes more coordinated. Participation in group activities with others in the litter is seen. Dominance/hierarchy games are played between littermates. The seventh week is the ideal time for puppies to go to their new home.

At the end of this stage, puppies begin to be more cautious, but they are still curious and will investigate anything.

What to do: During weeks 3 to 6, the puppies will still be with the breeder. There should be a clear distinction between sleeping and play areas, so that puppies can leave the nest to go to the toilet. Puppies kept in too small a space, one where there is no distinction between the areas or where they cannot get out of the nest box unaided, do not have the chance to practice appropriate toileting behavior. Puppies raised in this way can be difficult to housebreak.

The puppies' rate of mental development will now depend on the complexity of their environment. An assortment of different objects (for example, cardboard boxes, a large piece of hard leather, toys, or an old glove) should be placed in the pen with the puppies to provide complexity. It is also helpful to have a few low, wide steps for the puppies to practice on. These will help them to negotiate stairs later.

During this time, a variety of noises, sounds, and different floor surfaces should also be encountered. This will probably happen naturally for puppies raised in a home environment.

Puppies should be isolated occasionally from littermates and their mother, and there should be plenty of contact with humans, both adults and children. This is particularly important in the final week before the puppy goes to the new home, and at least five minutes of individual attention should be given to each puppy every day, no matter how many puppies there are in the litter.

During weeks 6 to 8, the puppy should be starting to settle in with its new family. Socialization will continue as the puppy experiences the novelty of its new home. Housebreaking should begin as soon as the puppy is brought home.

Third stage: weeks 8 to 12

Appropriate behaviors begin to be exhibited at appropriate times. The puppy has a very strong desire to please. If puppies are still in the litter, the hierarchy among littermates begins to be sorted out. If the puppy has gone to a new home, it will begin to assess its position in the new family.

What to do: Your puppy should be experiencing and enjoying a wide variety of situations and environments (see Chapter 6). He will start assessing members of his family to find out their position in the hierarchy and will begin to determine where he fits in. It is important that he gets the correct message about his place in the pack at this stage (see Chapter 8). Play is very important, and he will need to learn to play human games and to reduce and inhibit his play-biting (see Chapter 9).

Juvenile Period: 3 to 6 Months

The puppy is still dependent on its owner. In the early stages of this period, puppies are usually eager to please and will do whatever they believe their owners want them to do. During this period they will continue to learn about the hierarchy within the family and attempt to find their own position within that hierarchy.

Environmental awareness is increasing. They begin to explore farther afield but always stay within range of the security of the owner or familiar territory.

Chewing and mouthing behaviors are common to facilitate teething and to aid environmental exploration.

What to do: Training and good manners should be developed as the puppy becomes better able to concentrate and learn. The willingness-to-please of this age should be used to the full, as training will be more difficult later as the puppy becomes more independent. Games can become more advanced and can be used as a reward for training.

Full use should be made of this time to impress on the puppy that humans are higher in rank than he is. This needs to be done gently, but unquestionably (see Chapter 8).

Your puppy should experience many different environments. Socialization should continue and be developed as the puppy learns to cope with new situations.

Adolescence: 6 Months to 1 Year/18 Months

Puppies become much more independent and are likely to challenge authority. They reach sexual maturity; females come into heat, with associated behavioral changes, and males experience dramatic fluctuations in male hormone levels. Chewing behaviors continue to be a priority. Territorial behavior begins to appear as puppies become more mature.

What to do: This is possibly the most difficult period to live through and it is a time when many people give away their dogs. If you have laid down solid foundations of good behavior up to this point, adolescence will be less wearing. However, it will be a time when you wonder what has gone wrong. Try to remember that it does not last forever! (See Chapter 19 for help.)

Maturity: 1 Year/18 Months Onward

Your dog will now be physically mature, although he will have some filling out to do. His character is now fully formed even though some refinement will still be occurring. Young adults continue to develop in character and will finally settle down at about three years of age.

What to do: You can relax a bit now; your job is mostly done. Refinement and continuation of training is needed, but you should now be able to take it easy and enjoy the first of many happy years with your well-balanced, well-trained, sociable friend.

Summary

Age	Period	Development	What to do
0–2 wk.	Newborn	Sleeps, suckles.	
2–3 wk.	Transitional	Senses begin to operate.	Gentle handling
3–12 wk.	Socialization		
3–5 wk.	1st stage	Reacts to loud sounds, plays, eats solid food, leaves nest to toilet.	Give separate sleep and play areas, provide complex environment, plenty of human contact and contact with other dogs.
5–8 wk.	2nd stage	Weaning begins, hierarchy games played in litter.	Socialization continues, puppies leave for new home.
8–12 wk.	3rd stage	Independent exploratory behavior, begins assessment of position in pack.	Socialization continues. Puppy learns to play human games and learns about position in the pack.
3–6 mo.	Juvenile	Explores farther afield. Chewing is a priority.	Training and good manners are developed. Low status impressed on puppy. Socialization continues.
6–12/18 mo.	Adolescence	More independent. Sexual maturity reached. Territorial behavior begins.	Difficult time for owners. Continue with training; watch out for challenges to authority.
12/18 mo. onward			Relax and enjoy a well-balanced dog.

CHAPTER FIVE

LIVING WITH A NEW PUPPY: THE FIRST STEPS

First impressions really do count, so care must be taken when introducing a puppy to your children, dogs, and other pets. Great excitement is usually generated when a new puppy arrives home, particularly where children are concerned. Try to diffuse this as much as possible and keep introductions low-key, quickly distracting the other occupants of the house as soon as the first meeting is over to allow the puppy to explore and the excitement to subside.

Careful introductions to other members of the household will ensure your puppy starts off on the right foot (or paw)!

Children

It is helpful, especially if you have young children, to make a rule that the puppy is not to be picked up. This will enable him to learn that children are friendly and nice to be with. He cannot learn this if he is whisked off his feet and held in an awkward, unsupported way each time he meets them.

If you already have a dog, allow him and your new puppy time to investigate each other gradually, on neutral territory.

Also make it a rule that your puppy is not to be disturbed when sleeping. If you allow your children to treat your puppy like a new toy, you will end up with one very tired, irritable puppy. Buying the children a new game or toy at the same time as you bring the puppy home may help to distract their attention and gives the puppy some much-needed space to find its feet. After the first few days, the puppy will lose its novelty value for the children and they will begin to get used to their new friend.

Other Dogs

Introducing your puppy to any other dogs in your household is best done away from your home, while out on a walk. Exercise your dog well on the way to collect your puppy and keep them separate in the car. On the way home, take them both out to a new area, somewhere your dog has not been before and away from areas where other dogs have been (your puppy will not be fully protected by vaccination yet). Allow them to investigate each other. Try not to interfere too much, but distract them by moving to a new area if either looks unhappy with the situation. Your older dog will be distracted by the interesting new sights and smells and will probably not take much notice of the newcomer.

When you get home, repeat this procedure in the garden, taking the puppy in first. Then let your puppy into the house, bringing the older dog in afterward. Pick up any toys, bones, food dishes, beds, and blankets beforehand. Keep excitement to a minimum, and try not to interfere too much. If you are worried that your older dog may attack him, put your puppy in a playpen or indoor kennel so that both can investigate one another safely. Aggression toward puppies usually occurs because the older dog is frightened by the puppy running excitedly around its legs.

When they have settled down, replace beds and blankets, but keep toys and bones out of the way for a few days. Try to give the older dog more attention and affection than you did before the puppy came, and remind the children to do this too.

Cats

Usually, introductions between very young puppies and cats go quite smoothly. When introducing your puppy to an adult cat, restrain the puppy, not the cat. If you have a cat that stands up for itself, it will probably hiss and spit at the puppy to begin with, and the puppy will retreat. If your cat is the sort that will run away from the puppy, be ready to distract the puppy so that he is not tempted to give chase.

Teach your puppy that cats are not for chasing. Introductions can go well if you restrain your puppy rather than your cat.

Make sure that your puppy does not chase your cat. Continue to restrain him until the cat is accustomed to his presence and the puppy has learned that the cat is not there for chasing. During times when you are not there to supervise them, keep your puppy in his playpen (see page 45) so that the cat can stay right away from this area if it wishes.

Problems usually arise later, when the puppy is more confident. Often it will begin to bounce at the cat, having learned that this makes the cat run. If you see this beginning to happen, interrupt your puppy and offer a game with a toy instead. By doing this, you will be teaching him that cats are not for playing with and, instead, that humans are the source of all games. If necessary, attach a line to the puppy's collar and quickly stand on it to prevent your puppy chasing the cat whenever you see him preparing to do so and then distract him with a toy.

The First Night

It is helpful to make your puppy as sleepy as possible before he goes to bed. If he has had a long journey and has spent all day with his new family, the chances are that he will be tired anyway. Playing with him will help to use up the last of his energy, and feeding a warm, milky meal will also help. Remember to take him out to relieve himself for one last time before he finally settles down.

Before you collect your puppy from the breeder, take a small blanket and ask them to put it into the bed where the mother and puppies sleep for a few days (it gets very dirty and smelly!). Collect this with your puppy and seal it into a plastic bag. When your puppy goes to bed for the night, wrap this blanket around a warm hot-water bottle and put this into your puppy's bed; he will find this very reassuring and comforting because it smells familiar.

Opinions vary on how you should handle your puppy's first night with you. Some say that you should start as you mean to go on and simply put him to bed in the kitchen and ignore any howling or crying. If you decide on this course of action, do not respond to the noise your puppy is making. If you do, he will learn that making a noise is successful, and it will prolong the time he takes to tolerate being alone.

Puppies howl or cry when they are separated from whatever they are most attached to; initially this is their mother and littermates. When you bring your puppy home, this attachment transfers itself to you. Being isolated is not a natural state for animals that live in packs, and my view is that they should learn to be alone gradually.

During the first few nights, take him up to the bedroom with you and put him on a blanket in a high-sided cardboard box that he cannot climb out of. Any whimpering can be quietened by a reassuring pat or a quiet word. Do not over-fuss or respond to every murmur.

If he wakes up, cries loudly, and tries to get out in the middle of the night, he probably needs to go to relieve himself. Get up (even if it is 3 A.M. and raining) and walk him quickly outside to the garden. Praise and produce a tidbit if he goes, and take him back to his box until you are ready to get up (see Chapter 7 for housebreaking procedures).

After the first few nights, your puppy should be settled into your house and have become accustomed to being without his mother and littermates. He will also be getting used to being left alone (see Chapter 14). Consequently, by the end of the first week in your household, he should be ready to sleep on his own at night. He may be a bit unsettled for the first few nights in his new room, but do not go in to him if he howls or cries when you shut the door. Ignore him and he will soon get used to sleeping alone.

Before leaving him, it is useful to put down a large sheet of plastic, covered with several sheets of newspaper in case he needs to go to the toilet in the middle of the night. During the day, when he goes to the toilet in the garden, collect a small sample of his urine on a ball of cotton and keep it in a plastic bag. Dabbing this in the center of the sheets of newspaper will attract your puppy to it when he needs to go to the toilet during the night.

Some puppies will not want to go to the toilet in the house and, on waking up, make a lot of fuss in the middle of the night. If he does this, it is worth going down to let him out rather than force him to go on the floor. Do not give him any attention while you are down there; you are there to open the door and accompany him outside only. Otherwise he will begin to cry for you whenever he wakes up and finds himself alone. Only when he relieves himself outside should you give him attention and praise for doing the right thing.

A Puppy Playpen

This is an essential piece of equipment for bringing up a well-behaved puppy. Not only does it allow you to relax mentally and forget about your puppy for short periods — essential if you are not to get overtired and cross with him — but it also teaches him some self-control. Dogs in a human household have to learn to lie down and relax when no one wants to play or give them attention. When in the playpen, there are limited options for activity, and they quickly learn to settle down.

Playpens also prevent puppies from getting into all sorts of trouble while their owners are busy with something else. Puppies can learn many bad habits if they roam the house unchecked — such as chewing on electric wires or shoes and stealing cookies left out on the table — especially when there is no one home. Since you are not there to supervise, bad behavior goes uncorrected, and the behaviors you want are not encouraged.

A simple way to prevent this is to construct a puppy playpen. It can be as large as you like, but should be at least large enough to have a sleeping area and another part, covered with newspaper, where your puppy can get out of bed to go to the toilet if necessary.

You can achieve this by barricading off a corner of the room in some way. Make sure the partitions are secure and cannot fall on your puppy or trap him if he tries to escape. Alternatively, you can buy specially

made pens, often made of panels that are linked together. You can order these from good pet shops. For some puppies, you will need a lid to prevent them from climbing out when they get older.

Puppies can learn many bad habits if they are left to roam about the house alone. A playpen will give you some breathing space and your puppy a place to settle down.

The best place for the playpen is usually in the kitchen. In most households, this is the place where people congregate and pass through and where there is usually something happening most of the time. Your puppy can then get used to many different sights, sounds, and smells from the safety of his playpen. In addition, kitchens usually have a, easily washable floor, which is useful should there be problems during the housebreaking period. If you have a small kitchen, it is better to give the puppy a smaller pen than to put him in a larger one in a room where few people pass by and where there is little activity.

Put your puppy's bed in the playpen with one or two chews and toys. He can then be safely left there whenever you go out or whenever you cannot concentrate on him. When your puppy is allowed out, you are there to teach him right from wrong. The training process is then much quicker, because your puppy is never rewarded for unacceptable behavior and will very rapidly learn to show only the behaviors you want. Once your puppy has learned right from wrong and behaves well in the house, even when left alone, you can dispense with the pen.

Not a punishment

Do not use the pen as a prison when your puppy has done something wrong. If he does something you do not like, simply correct him, show him what you want him to do, and praise him for being good. The pen should not be associated with punishment. Frequently talk to your puppy when he is in the pen and, if it is big enough, play with him in it so that he enjoys being there.

Do not keep your puppy in the pen for long periods. The pen is meant only as a safe place to keep your puppy while you are engaged elsewhere. He should be given as much time and attention outside the pen as you can manage, and he should not be left there all day.

Introducing the pen

If you introduce the pen at a very early age, your puppy will accept it as part of life. If you have an older puppy, start by leaving the pen open, putting his bed inside and encouraging him to go and rest there when he is tired. Throw tidbits and toys into the pen and praise and play with him whenever he goes in there of his own accord. It is much better if he goes in of his own free will rather than having to be forced to do so each time. After a few days, when he is happy to go inside, you can begin to confine him there whenever you need to.

Barking in the pen

Do not, on any account, take your puppy out of the pen, tell him off, talk to him, or look at him if he barks or whines. Do not pay him any attention at all until he is quiet again. If you do, you will be reinforcing this behavior, and he will quickly learn that he can get his freedom by barking incessantly.

After a few minutes of quiet, you may decide that it is time to let him out for a game or to go to the toilet, but it should be your decision, not his. The only possible exception to this is if you think he needs to go outside to go to the toilet. If so, wait until the barking or whining ceases and then whisk him outside quickly. Otherwise, make it a rule that he comes out of the pen only when he has been well-behaved.

A retreat from children

If you have young children, your puppy can easily become overexcited, and play sessions can get out of hand. Using a playpen means that when the puppy is allowed out, you are there to supervise, teach "good" games, and prevent play-biting. It also ensures that the children do not tease the puppy or teach it bad habits.

Puppies need quite a lot of sleep, especially when young, and an overstimulated, overexcited, and overtired puppy is likely to become irritable and snappy. Judicious use of the pen can prevent this. Your puppy can be put there to rest periodically, and once he has learned he cannot get out to play, he will quickly settle down and sleep.

Your puppy will also need to learn that he cannot join in all of the children's games and that, sometimes, he has to sit quietly while they play. The playpen is an ideal way of achieving this.

Some puppies will want to go to the pen to rest when they are tired and the children become too much. Leave the pen open if possible, and make sure the children know that the pen is off-limits

Indoor Kennel

If you do not have enough space for a playpen, or cannot construct one, an alternative is to use an indoor kennel or travelling cage. This is a small mesh cage (it should be as large as possible and at least large enough to enable your puppy to stand up, lie down, and turn around comfortably once fully grown).

The big disadvantage is that there is nowhere for your puppy to go to relieve himself, and it cannot exercise or explore in it. This means that you cannot leave your puppy there for more than an hour at a time, so that its use is limited. However, an indoor kennel is better than having nowhere at all to confine your puppy while you are involved in something else. Just be careful about the amount of time your puppy is left in it, and do not put him there unless he is tired and sleepy, and has recently been outside.

The Use of a Stairgate

Stairgates (also known as baby-gates) can be useful devices, especially if you have young children as well. They can be used when you do not want your puppy to be in the same room with you — for example, when you are playing with your baby on the floor or you have important visitors that you want to concentrate on. The puppy can still have your company but can be safely kept away from whatever is going on, by putting him behind the stairgate.

Routine

Stairgates can be very useful — your puppy can see you but can be kept out of the way until you want him to join you.

It is important to establish a routine for your puppy. Dogs are very much creatures of habit, and they will adjust to life in your household much more easily if there is some sort of order to their lives. Keeping to a routine will also be easier for you because it allows you to cope with everyday chores, such as housebreaking, without having to think too much about them. Having a written routine to follow may help to ensure that, in a busy household, your puppy's needs will not be overlooked or forgotten.

The following routine is for a very young puppy. You may find that this plan does not suit your household or your puppy, but it should give you some ideas to enable you to design your own. The routine is a basis for what happens each day. It is flexible, to allow you to live your own lives around it, but it should be kept to as much as possible to allow for housebreaking, feeding, and for such essentials, as play, socialization, and grooming. The routine may look complicated and time consuming, but it makes everything easier in the long run. For example, it may seem unnecessary to take your puppy out to the toilet each hour.

However, taking him out regularly is easier than cleaning up accidents, and he will learn in a much shorter time.

Suggested Daily Routine

Morning

8	Wake up. Out for walk. Short play session.
8:30	Family breakfast.
9	Puppy's breakfast.
9:15	Out for walk. Short play session. Rest period.
10	Out for walk. Play/training session. Rest period.
11	Out for walk. Socialization time.

Afternoon

12	Out for walk. Family lunch.
1	Puppy's second meal.
1:15	Out for walk. Rest period.
2	Out for walk. Short play session. Rest period.
3	Out for walk. Supervised freedom of the house. Play time.
4	Out for walk. Rest period.
5	Puppy's third meal.
5:15	Out for walk. Rest period.

Evening

6	Play/training session. Out for walk.
7	Family dinner. Rest period.
8	Out for walk. Socialization time. Handling/grooming session.
9	Puppy's fourth meal.
9:15	Out for walk. Play/training session. Supervised freedom of the house.
10	Out for walk. Vigorous play session.
11	Out for walk. Bed.

Introduction to Collar and Leash

When your puppy has had a few days to settle into your household, it will be time to get him used to wearing a collar. Buy a suitably sized buckle collar (never a check chain or half-check collar). It needs to be large enough to enable you to insert two fingers between the collar and his neck when put on.

Put it on just before something pleasant is to happen to your puppy — for example, when you are about to play with him, take him outside, or feed him. He will probably frantically attempt to scratch it off at first. Ignore this and praise him as soon as he stops. After a few moments, distract his attention from his collar with the next event. Take it off during this event and put it on again later.

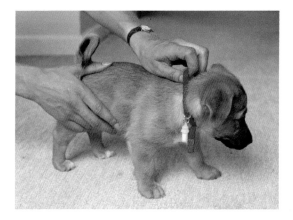

Once your puppy is used to his collar, teach him to tolerate being restrained by it by holding it firmly while you hold his body with your free hand to prevent him from twisting.

After a few days of this, he will get used to the collar and begin to ignore it. It can then be left on all the time. Puppies can easily get lost, so attach an identification tag to it. Remember that puppies grow at a tremendous rate, so check the collar every few days to be sure that it still fits well.

Later, as your puppy becomes used to being restrained and handled, begin to accustom him to being restrained gently by his collar. Initially hold his body with your free hand to prevent him from swiveling around and trying to pull away from you, twisting your fingers in the collar as he does so. Ignore any wriggling and praise him when he stands still. Gentle, firm restraint in this way will soon teach him that he cannot get away if someone takes hold of his collar, and he will learn to accept it.

When he is used to being restrained by the collar, attach a leash and let it drag around after him during a few play sessions so that he becomes used to the feel of it. Pick up the end of the leash sometimes, but keep still when you do this. Your puppy needs to learn that being on the leash means that he is fastened to his owner and cannot go where he wants to any more. When your puppy has accepted the restraint, praise him and let him go free again.

CHAPTER SIX

SOCIALIZATION

During the early part of a puppy's life, new objects are approached with curiosity and without fear. New experiences are tolerated with a similar lack of concern. In the wild, wolf pups can learn about their surroundings more quickly if they have no fear, and it makes sense for them to be unafraid while they are still under the protection of their mother and other members of the pack. As the pups mature and wander off to explore on their own, they tend to be cautious of situations and objects that they have not been familiarized with. Dogs have inherited this ability, to a greater or lesser extent depending on what breed they are, from their wild ancestors and, as they get older, puppies become more cautious. Anything that has not been encountered before will be met with suspicion and fear.

The more new experiences and enjoyable encounters that a puppy has as it grows up, the more likely it will be to mature into a well-adjusted adult that can take anything in its stride without becoming fearful. This process is called socialization. Socialization is *the* most important process in a puppy's life, and how much of it you do or fail to do will be reflected directly in the future character of your puppy. Undersocialized puppies grow up shy, fearful, sometimes aggressive, and unable to live their lives to the full.

If you do nothing else, you owe it to your puppy to find time for socialization. It is not difficult to do, but time must be set aside for it. It is probably the most important factor on the future well-being of your dog and in the formation of a well-balanced, friendly adult.

When to Socialize

One of the major differences between ourselves and dogs is the speed at which we grow up. It takes a human approximately 18 to 21 years to mature (although I have known it to take longer!), whereas dogs mature in about one to one-and-a-half years. A week in our childhood is a relatively short period, whereas to a puppy it represents a large proportion of its puppyhood.

It is therefore important that you make the most of puppyhood and pack in as many good experiences as possible during this time. Deep and lasting impressions are formed at this age and, good or bad, they will be remembered throughout a dog's life.

Research has shown that, from the age of three to four weeks, puppies are capable of learning from their experiences, and the more pleasant experiences a puppy has before the age of 12 weeks, the more confident he will be in new situations. Older puppies are more cautious and find it more difficult to become accustomed to new experiences. Therefore, give him many enjoyable encounters as early as possible.

Socialization should be a continuous process up to the age of maturity, and concentrated effort should be put in until this age. Socialization becomes progressively more difficult as the puppy grows older, but it is still worth doing and adult dogs may need further effort in order to socialize them adequately.

The Breeder's Role

By the time your puppy is weaned and ready to leave its mother, the process of socialization should have already begun. When the puppy is ready to move to its new home at six to eight weeks, about one month of prime socialization time has already gone by. The breeder, therefore, has a responsibility to ensure that puppies are well handled and socialized during that time. This is why you need to make a careful choice about where

Novel objects are approached by young puppies with curiosity. Early experiences like these help to broaden the puppy's outlook and develop his awareness.

your puppy comes from. If you obtain a puppy from a breeder who has not socialized the dog adequately, you will have to make up for lost time and work very hard at your socialization program.

Your Role — Starting Right Away

The most usual ages for vaccinating a puppy are 8 and 12 weeks (sometimes 16 weeks as well). But bear in mind that until the vaccinations have taken effect, your puppy will be at risk of contracting diseases from other dogs.

Puppies can be vaccinated at six weeks of age, but because the success of this vaccination cannot be guaranteed, veterinaries are reluctant to put owners to the extra expense. The reason early vaccination cannot be guaranteed is that if any immunity acquired from the mother is still present, the two systems cancel each other out and the

Infection may occur if your puppy is in contact with unvaccinated dogs or exposed to areas where they have soiled the ground. Taking your puppy out in your arms to avoid contact with the ground may be one option.

puppy is left unprotected. The amount of maternal immunity left varies with the individual puppy and cannot easily be tested.

However, vaccines are now being produced which allow puppies to be vaccinated at the age of six weeks with a reasonable chance of success. Puppies that will eventually become guide dogs for the blind, for example, are given early vaccinations so that the puppy walkers can take them out from the age of six weeks. This enables them to receive maximum benefit from a socialization program and gives them a head start on puppies that are kept inside until they are fully vaccinated at 13 to 16 weeks.

Early vaccination tends to be a more expensive option, but I strongly recommend it, since the benefits of early socialization are so great. Talk to your veterinary about the options available. His knowledge of the latest vaccines and local disease conditions will allow you to make an informed decision.

My view is that a compromise is necessary between the protection of physical and mental health. Early vaccination at six weeks will give you the best chance of protecting your puppy before the later vaccinations take effect. Taking him out and about but taking reasonable precautions to ensure he is not exposed to disease will allow him to socialize before he is fully covered. Otherwise, you will lose weeks of vital socialization time, which could make the difference between a shy, fearful adult and a well-adjusted, friendly one.

Protection From Bad Experiences

When you take on a puppy, you assume the role of parent and pack leader, and therefore, during your puppy's early life, it is up to you to protect him from bad experiences. This does not mean that you should overprotect him, but it does mean you will need to think about the way he is viewing a given situation and, if necessary, modify his experience so that he does not become fearful.

It would not be sensible, for example, to allow him to run up to a strange dog without first finding out if the dog is good with puppies. The dog might turn on your puppy, giving him a fright, that if not countered by good experiences, would leave a permanent mental scar.

Carefully observing your puppy's reactions will help you to tell if he is even mildly fearful. Watch his ears and his tail and his body posture. Is he trying to make himself smaller by lowering his tail and ears and by crouching? Some puppies will not show these signs so obviously but will try to escape from the source of the fear if possible. Is he straining to get away but being restrained by his leash? By carefully watching your puppy at other times, as well as when you are in a difficult situation, you will soon be able to read the signs and understand what your puppy is feeling.

At a puppy's head height (left), his line of view is significantly different from ours. He has little knowledge of the world around him, so try to build up new experiences gradually.

At an adult's head height (right) a puppy appears small and vulnerable.

If your puppy is showing signs of apprehension or is already fearful, tone down the new experience so that your puppy is no longer afraid. In practice, this can mean putting more distance between yourselves and the situation or removing one of the new elements. For example, if your puppy has not met children before, four noisy children may be over-whelming; restrict the encounter to one quiet child at first.

Do not act sympathetically if your puppy becomes apprehensive. Showing your concern will cause him to think that there is something to be afraid of. Instead, try to jolly him along and look as if you are having a good time and are not worried and, at the same time, change the situation so that your puppy has less to be apprehensive about.

Games with toys, or feeding tidbits, can help to speed up the process and allow your puppy to feel at home with the new situation more quickly. If strangers produce tidbits or play games with your puppy, they will often be accepted more readily. If your puppy will not play or eat in a new situation, he is probably feeling too much anxiety, and you will need to do something to help reduce it. If he is just at the border of what he is able to cope with, playing with him and feeding may help him to relax.

When you know your puppy's limits, extend them each day. Expose him to as much of a new situation as he can cope with without becoming scared. Encourage him to enjoy the experience with food and games. His limits will extend every day, and he will soon become unafraid.

The more situations your puppy is familiar with, the less time he will take to adjust to new encounters. If your puppy is afraid of passing cars, find a place where you can stand some distance from the road. When you sense a little apprehension, stop and play a game with your puppy (keeping him on his leash), feed him tidbits, and talk to him until he is playing happily and having a good time. Repeat as often as possible over a few days, getting closer to the road each time, until he is not afraid to stand at the roadside. Never go beyond your puppy's limit.

What to Do in Case of a Bad Experience

If, despite your careful supervision, your puppy does have a bad experience, it is important to put this right as soon as possible by arranging for your puppy to encounter the same situation again, but this time for it to be a pleasant event. Several of these pleasant encounters will be needed to overcome the unpleasant one. How many will depend on how shy your puppy is; timid puppies will need more pleasant events than outgoing puppies to overcome an unpleasant experience.

Encounters with cars passing close are too much for this puppy. Further encounters will be needed, but stand away from the road at first and distract him with tidbits and games to make the experience more pleasant.

How to Socialize Successfully

The secret to good socialization is to try to look at the world from your puppy's point of view. Try to imagine what it is like to be that small and vulnerable and to have such a limited knowledge. Do not overwhelm him with too much all at once but start with brief encounters and slowly build up until he is experiencing more and more. Ensure that he enjoys each new experience, playing with him and talking happily to him so that he knows there is nothing to be worried about. His natural curiosity will make him want to explore new situations and, provided that you protect him from becoming afraid, he should become more and more confident as he gains experience.

Humans

Humans come in all shapes, sizes, ages, and characters. Your dog will rapidly get used to people he sees every day or who regularly visit your house, but he will be unfamiliar with others unless you take care to expose him to them. It is easy to forget this because we have been familiarized with many different types of people as we have grown up.

If you want your dog to be 100 percent confident of all humans, you will need to introduce him to all sorts of people. This includes those wearing glasses, beards, unusual clothing, uniforms, hats, motorcycle helmets, carrying bags or sacks, people in wheel-chairs, people who walk with a limp or who use canes, and people of different races.

Your puppy needs to learn not to be frightened of eye contact with humans. You can speed up the process by holding something that the puppy wants under your chin until he looks into your eyes. Smile at the same time, showing your teeth. While your puppy is looking up at you, give him the treat.

Exposure to people needs to be both at home, on your own territory, and off territory in parks, towns, on the street, and in other people's homes. Your puppy needs to get used to people running or jogging, playing football, riding bikes, and all the other strange activities that humans engage in!

Familiarizing your puppy with all sorts of people engaged in all sorts of activities is still not enough. People, especially dog lovers, are prone to stopping, to look at your dog and approaching. For a dog that has not learned that such approaches are friendly, that behavior can be very frightening. Puppies need to learn that a human approaching with wide-open eyes and displaying a full set of teeth in a smile is nothing to be afraid of! Familiarizing your puppy with this aspect of human behavior is very important.

Until your puppy has learned this lesson, ask people to look away if they are frightening him by staring at him, even if they are doing it unintentionally, or distract their attention from him by speaking to them. This takes the pressure off the puppy and allows him to relax. Given time, your puppy's natural curiosity will encourage him to come forward and make friends.

Gradually build up the time that he can hold your gaze, talking kindly to him all the time until you give him the treat. When he is happy with this exercise, you can ask strangers to do the same.

Humans are also apt to touch unfamiliar dogs, especially if they own dogs themselves. Handling exercises to do with your own puppy will be covered later, but it is important to ensure that your dog is happy to allow strangers, both adults and children, to touch him all over.

Inviting friends to your house while your puppy is still young is one of the best ways to socialize a puppy with humans. If he is shy, allow him to come out in his own time; do not try to force the issue or you will make him worse. Tell any well-meaning people approaching him too quickly that your puppy should make the first move. Smelly, tasty tidbits given by the visitor can help to overcome any fear he may have.

Invite people who are not keen on dogs or who do not know how to handle them as well as those who do. People who are unfamiliar with

Your puppy should meet children of all ages. Children are naturally attracted to puppies, and you need to ensure that your puppy is not overwhelmed by them. Give children tidbits to give to him so that the experience is a rewarding one. Teach them to stroke him under the chin rather than patting their hands on his head, which could feel threatening.

dogs tend to approach them differently from those that are familiar and it is wise to accustom your puppy to all types of people.

It is particularly important to get your puppy used to children of all ages, especially if you do not have children of your own. Even if you do, he will need to accept other people's children who are different ages from yours and who will have different temperaments and personalities. Try to see that your puppy meets babies, toddlers, infants, juniors, and teenagers.

One of the easiest ways to do this is to walk your puppy to a local school and back at the appropriate times, even if you do not have children yourself. Children are naturally attracted to puppies, which makes it easy for you to get the two of them together, but take steps to ensure that your puppy is not overwhelmed by the experience should the numbers get too great. Again, giving children tasty tidbits to offer to him (show them how, so they do not get their fingers bitten) can make the experience pleasant for your puppy and he will begin to look forward to meeting them. Allow him time to get to know one or two of the children so that he accumulates friends of different ages. Take toys with you so that the children can play with him.

Taking your puppy to children's play areas allows him to become used to the sight and sound of children playing, running, and screaming.

Teaching him to remain calm in these situations and not to join in is a valuable lesson. It will help to prevent later misunderstandings where your dog may run after and jump up at a child in play, possibly bringing the child to the ground. Being chased by a dog, even if the dog is just playing, can be a very frightening experience for a child, particularly if they are not used to dogs or if the animal is larger than they are.

Make sure that your puppy has been exercised and allowed time to go to the toilet before you get to the children's play area, and clean up after him if he should mess in the vicinity. Talk to your vet about an adequate worming program for your puppy so that he does not pose a public health risk.

Other Dogs

Great care should be taken when introducing your puppy to adult dogs. Do not do so unless you know that the dogs have been well socialized themselves and are used to meeting unfamiliar puppies.

This does not, however, mean that you should keep your puppy away from all dogs. Doing this could be just as harmful, because he will then be undersocialized with other dogs and uncertain of how to act around them. This uncertainty could lead to aggression later. Instead, it is important to find other dogs that you know will be good with him.

Take care when walking your puppy where other dogs are loose. A confident dog running up to a shy puppy can terrify him, even though it means no harm. If the puppy is restricted by a leash, he may be more frightened, or if he is loose he may run away, which could be worse. A fright like this can leave a permanent mental scar. Protect your puppy from such encounters if he is shy and see that he receives more socialization with other friendly adult dogs under controlled conditions.

By keeping away from unfamiliar dogs in the park, unless you know them to be safe, and encouraging your puppy to play games with you instead, many frightening encounters with other dogs can be avoided. In this way, all experiences with other dogs are positive, and your puppy will have no reason to be aggressive toward them later on.

Puppy socialization classes

One of the best ways for puppies to build on their knowledge of dog communication systems, which they began in the litter, is for them to attend a well-run puppy socialization class.

Your puppy can start to attend these classes when he is between the ages of 12 and 18 weeks (older puppies who may inhibit the younger ones or play too roughly are not allowed) or sometimes earlier, especially if the classes are run at a veterinarian's. These classes are a relatively new idea, but are becoming more and more popular because they

A puppy socialization class is one of the best ways for your puppy to learn more about dog communication systems.

are so beneficial. Before joining, it is sensible to go along to watch a class in progress.

All training at the class should use reward methods *only*. Do not attend if pulling and pushing of puppies is recommended. The classes should not be a free-for-all where puppies play together all the time. Instead, the owners should be constantly communicating with their own puppy during the periods of free-play with the other puppies in the group. Learning to come away from a play-session when called is one of the things that should be taught to puppies in such classes.

By attending puppy classes, your puppy will continue to learn the body language and signals necessary for adequate communication with other dogs in a low-risk environment. During play sessions he will learn to inhibit his biting and learn other valuable lessons that he would have acquired had he stayed in his litter. You will, in turn, learn how to train him and also how to understand him better.

Contact with adult dogs is needed in addition to these classes. Puppies should learn that not every dog is available for play all the time.

A friendly adult dog will firmly teach your puppy respect for others without becoming aggressive, but finding suitable dogs can be difficult.

A New Environment, Situation, Object, or Event

Puppies should be familiarized with anything that they are likely to encounter in their adult life. This includes anything that may appear frightening, such as vacuum cleaners, washing machines, even large plastic bags blowing in the wind.

Vehicles — including cars, bicycles, and trucks — which are ordinary to us, can seem like huge roaring monsters to a new puppy out for the first time, and any apprehension he may have will need to be overcome.

Take your puppy into all types of situations that may be useful later on. If you do not have a car, try to borrow one so that he becomes used to riding in it. If you do not usually use public transportation, make a point of taking him on buses and trains. This could be very useful later when the car breaks down!

If you live in town, take outings to the country so that he can get used to livestock and horses. Teaching a puppy how to behave around "prey" animals will prevent him from wanting to chase them. If a puppy is brought up with sheep, for example, and prevented from giving chase, he will learn to accept that they are boring creatures that do not run. If he walks past many cats in their gardens while he is on a leash and is not allowed to frighten them, he will learn that they do not run and are not for chasing. Similarly, if joggers routinely run past him while he is a puppy and he is prevented from giving chase, he will get used to them.

Try to accustom your puppy to anything he will be exposed to in later life, but keep him under control so that he cannot give chase. Doing this badly is slightly worse than not doing it at all. For example, if your puppy meets sheep on a few occasions while off the leash, learns that

Contact with adult dogs is important. A friendly adult dog will gently teach your puppy respect.

they run and is excited by them, he will become excited whenever he sees them as an adult and will want to give chase. A dog that has never seen sheep as a puppy may not know that they are fun to chase and will ignore them until he sees them moving.

If you decide to socialize a puppy with sheep or any other potential prey animal, ensure that he sees so many of them while he is under control that he becomes bored with them. Take him to an area where he can see them and keep him at a distance that does not cause them to run away. Keep him on the leash (an extending leash if you have one), play games, and train him. This will keep the excitement centered on you rather than on the animals. Several sessions should be enough to teach him that other animals are boring, but that when they are around, *you* become very interesting. In this way, your puppy will want to be with you on a walk rather than running off and chasing animals.

If you live in the country, go to town. Visit a dog-friendly store and take any opportunity to go to country fairs, where your puppy can have a wide variety of different experiences. If your puppy shows apprehension of anything, whether it is objects, situations or events, work on them specifically until any fear disappears.

The Appendix at the end of this book gives a socialization program for your puppy. Use it or design your own, so that you have a structured plan to work with and stick to. This will help to keep you from putting off socialization sessions in favor of something that you may want to do instead. Your puppy should come first — you can never get this time in your puppy's life back again.

The Shy Puppy

How shy a young puppy is, and hence how much socialization he requires, will depend partly on his genetic makeup and partly on the environment he has found himself in during his short life.

Shyness seems to be an inherited trait, and your puppy will have inherited the predisposition to be afraid of the unfamiliar to a greater or lesser extent depending on the breed to which he belongs. Sensitive breeds, such as Collies and German Shepherd Dogs, seem to be more shy and to need much more socialization than robust breeds, such as Labradors and Springers. Shyness seems to be linked to mental sensitivity, and the more sensitive the breed, the more need there will be to socialize the puppy.

If you have a quiet family with few comings and goings, your puppy is likely to be shyer than one that lives in a lively household. Whether or not you have taken your puppy out in the early weeks or whether you kept him at home will also have an effect.

Whatever your puppy's background, you will need to be aware of how shy he is and watch him carefully while he encounters situations

If your puppy is very shy with strangers, let him make the first move rather than increasing his fear by dragging him to them. Ask them to avoid eye contact, keep as still as possible, turn sideways to the puppy, and make themselves as small as possible by crouching or sitting on the floor. Natural curiosity will make your puppy want to approach. Ask people to talk quietly to him without looking at him and to offer him tasty tidbits.

for the first time. Is he moving from or toward an object or person? Is he looking around calmly, or does he focus on any new sound rapidly and with some degree of alarm?

If you own a shy puppy, it would be wise to invest a lot of time in socialization as soon as possible in the puppy's life. A dog is never too old to socialize, but it does become progressively more difficult as he grows older.

Given time, your puppy will begin to relax and enjoy the company of strangers. You will need to work extensively on a very shy puppy and make very sure that he is happy with all types of people approaching him, calling his name, and staring at him before you begin to relax his socialization program.

CHAPTER SEVEN

HOUSEBREAKING: THE FIRST LESSON

Most animals that are born in a nest have an instinctive desire to move away from the nest to relieve themselves. They will do so, without being taught, as soon as they are able. Dogs are no exception, and at the age of about three weeks, they will begin to leave the sleeping area to urinate. They are, as it were, preprogramed to be housebroken; we just have to teach them that houses are our nests, and that they have to move outside when they want to relieve themselves.

Take your puppy outside to the same spot in your yard or garden at the following times:

- shortly after each feeding
- after playing
- after exercise
- after any excitement (e.g., visitors arriving)
- immediately upon waking
- first thing in the morning
- last thing at night
- at least once every hour

From the age of about three weeks, puppies will instinctively leave the nest in order to relieve themselves. They are "preprogramed" to be housebroken.

Allowing him to wander around and sniff at the ground will help to speed up the process. It is important to stay outside with him. Take a coat if it is cold, or an umbrella if it is raining, so you are not in a hurry to go back in.

Be patient and wait. As soon as he begins, say a chosen phrase to him. Choose anything you can say easily in a public place (you may need to say it when people are listening), such as "Be clean!". When he has finished,

*Take your puppy outside
to the same spot in your yard.
Stay with him and when he
begins, say a chosen phrase.
When he has finished, praise
him and play a game.*

praise enthusiastically (make that tail wag!) and play a game with him. Keep the area clean by picking up any mess and burying it or flushing it down the toilet.

Puppies are easily distracted when outside, so having the patience to stay with him until he has settled down is essential. If you leave him to it, he will probably run to the back door and spend the rest of the time trying to get back in with you. Once you let him in, the stress of the separation, together with the increased excitement and exercise, will make him want to go, and you will be left with a mess inside and an uneducated puppy.

Although you need to remain with him, there is no need to stay outdoors for hours, waiting for him to go. Wait for a few minutes only, and if nothing happens, take him inside and try again a little later.

If at any time of the day you notice your puppy sniffing the floor and circling or getting ready to squat, immediately interrupt him and take him outside. Let him walk. Do not pick him up, or he will not learn the vital link in the process, which is: "When I need to go, I need to get to the back door and into the garden."

If, at any time, you catch him in the act of going in the house, *shout!* What you shout is immaterial, but it needs to be loud enough to capture his undivided attention and to stop him mid-flow, but not so loud that he runs for cover. Do not punish or get angry; the distress this causes your puppy will inhibit the learning process. He will also begin to avoid going to the toilet in front of you because he knows it makes you angry and will sneak away to do it, making it harder for you to teach him the correct behavior.

As soon as you have shouted, run away from him, toward the back door, calling him happily and enthusiastically to encourage him to follow. Go outside to your chosen spot and wait until he has relaxed and finished what he started earlier. Say your chosen phrase as he goes, praise him, and play with him as usual. Take him back into the house and put him in another room while you clean up any mess.

At the times when you cannot concentrate on your puppy, it is best to keep him confined to a smaller area where accidents are not too important. If you are using a puppy playpen, cover the floor with a large sheet of plastic topped with newspaper so that accidents can be cleared up easily. If accidents do occur, consider it your fault and take your puppy out more frequently.

By following these simple procedures, your puppy will learn that the place to go to the toilet is outside and will get into good habits. The more frequently you take him out at the appropriate time and the fewer times he goes indoors, the quicker he will learn. Regular habits take time to develop, though, so be prepared for the occasional accident.

If you catch your puppy sniffing the floor, circling, and getting ready to squat, immediately interrupt him and walk him outside (do not pick him up).

Once he has formed the correct habit, he will begin to show signs of wanting to go out whenever he feels the need to go. Watch for signs like running to the door and back, or whining at the door, or pawing at it, and let him out. You can then begin to teach him how you want him to signal his need to be let out, by reinforcing one particular action more than the others.

Accidents Will Happen

Toileting inside will leave traces of scent on the floor that your puppy, with his ultrasensitive nose, will be able to detect long after you have disinfected and cleaned the area to your satisfaction. This will encourage him to use the spot again. To minimize this, use one of the following to clean the area:
• Odor eliminator — a special product available from veterinarians.
• Hot biological washing powder solution.
Ordinary household disinfectants mask the smell from us, but not from your puppy. They also contain chemicals that are thought to attract the dog back to the same place. A solution of white vinegar and water rubbed over the area can help to remove any stain from carpets.

What to Do at Night

Puppies, like children, have only a limited control over their bodies. Generally, when they feel the need to urinate, they have to go right away. Expecting them to last through a 6- to 8-hour night is too much and puppies can be seven or eight months old before they are completely clean.

In order to make sure that no messes are left on the floor, cover the whole area with a sheet of plastic and newspapers once you begin leaving him on his own at night. The plastic will prevent any waste matter from leaking through, thereby preventing smells on the floor, which would encourage this habit during the day.

If you have a puppy that wakes you up when he feels the need to go out rather than mess on the floor, it is worthwhile to get up. It will not be long before he can hold on all night.

Delayed Punishment — Why it Does Not Work

Never, ever punish your puppy if you find a mess on the floor that was done earlier. He will not learn from this, not because he cannot remember what he has done, but because he cannot relate the punishment he is receiving with the earlier act of going to the toilet on the floor. As soon as you begin to look angry, your puppy will display a submissive response in order to appease you and turn off your anger. Unfortunately for puppies, the submissive response looks to us like guilt, so we are inclined to punish more, thinking to ourselves "he knows he has done wrong because he is looking guilty."

Not only is punishing after the event ineffective, it may also be counterproductive. If your puppy lives in fear of you suddenly becoming aggressive for no apparent reason, he will be insecure and unhappy, which may inhibit his learning ability. Worse still, if you punish him when returning to the room, he may begin to become anxious about being left alone, which may cause him to show all sorts of unwanted behaviors when he is older.

How Long Will it Take?

Different puppies learn at different rates. Some pick up what is required almost instantly, others may take much longer. Some take as long as six months or more. A puppy that came from a dirty or cramped kennel is likely to take longer than one that had a better start. Bright puppies will learn more quickly than less intelligent ones.

The biggest influence on how quickly a puppy becomes housebroken is how much time and effort you put in. More input from you will speed up the time taken to become completely clean; less input will prolong the process.

Toilet Training on Command

Toilet training should not end with housebreaking. About 34.6 million dogs live in this country, many in towns and built-up areas. As pressure on available space becomes greater, the public is becoming increasingly conscious of the problems of dog fouling, especially on sidewalks and areas where children play.

If you want to avoid the fairly unpleasant but necessary task of picking up after your dog in the street, it makes sense to train your dog to go before you leave home. This is not as difficult as it may seem but requires a fair amount of patience in the early stages.

If you have been successfully working at the housebreaking process, you will, by the time you are able to take your fully vaccinated puppy out, have a particular phrase that your puppy will associate with going to the toilet.

You should also have a fairly regular routine and will have some idea of when your puppy needs to go. Try to arrange your first walk to coincide with this time. Go out to the yard as usual, repeating your chosen phrase until your puppy does what is required. Praise enthusiastically and then take him out for a walk. If he does not go to the toilet, take him back inside for a while and try again later.

If you take your dog out for a walk only *after* he has been to the toilet, he will eventually begin to realize that producing the required deposit results in a walk.

This process takes patience to begin with, but your time and effort will be rewarded when you see other people picking up their dog's mess in the street, or you step in some that an irresponsible owner has left behind, and realize how easy your dog is to live with.

If your puppy needs to go again when out on a walk, despite having gone earlier in the garden, train him to use the gutter rather than the sidewalk. When you see him wanting to go, encourage him into the gutter (make sure no cars are coming first) and repeat your chosen phrase. Praise him when he has finished, before picking up the mess and disposing of it.

Living in an Apartment With no Garden

Housebreaking a puppy in an apartment that has no yard is more diffi-cult, but it is not impossible. An area that your puppy can use as a toilet area will need to be found close to the apartment. Since this may be a considerable distance for your puppy to walk, it becomes even more important that you take him out every hour without fail, to enable him to go outside. You will also need to be extra vigilant to your puppy's signs of wanting to relieve himself well in advance.

An alternative is to place plastic and newspaper just outside the door and train your puppy to go there. The major disadvantage, however, is that you will need to train him to go somewhere else later, once he has more control over his body.

Not Clean at Night?

Many young puppies ask to go out during the day when their owners are there, but are not clean during the night or if they are left for any length of time during the day. This is because immature animals need time to develop full control over their bodies and, when they need to relieve themselves, they simply cannot hold on until you come back. Owners often worry about this and think that their dog will never be clean when left alone.

There is no need to worry. Puppies take different lengths of time to learn control, but they all get there in the end. Until that time comes, ensure that your puppy is always left with plastic on the floor covered with newspaper and a spot of his previously collected urine dabbed in the center.

You will probably find that messing on the paper becomes less and less frequent as your pup gets older and develops more control. He should be completely clean by the time he is seven or eight months old.

If your dog reaches seven to eight months and is still not clean at night, it could be that he has developed a habit of going to the toilet at a particular time of the night. This can be cured by taking your puppy and his bed up to your bedroom and confining him to his bed so that he cannot get out. When he wakes up at his usual time and finds he cannot get out, he will whine and wake you up. Take him into the garden and allow him to relieve himself.

The next night, wait for 10 minutes before allowing him out. The following night he should wake up slightly later and again wait 10 minutes before getting up. Eventually he will have retrained his body to last all night without the need to go out (this does not take as long as you might imagine) and once he has acquired the habit of being clean all night he can be returned to the kitchen. Make sure you have thoroughly cleaned the kitchen floor (see above) before you do so.

Occasional Lapses

It is not uncommon for housebreaking to break down at some stage if the puppy is put under stress of any kind. This can happen if he is punished unpredictably, if he is unwell, or if there is a sudden change in family stability, such as Christmas, quarrels, or any sudden change of attitude toward the puppy for whatever reason. Bodily changes as your puppy reaches sexual maturity can also cause a short lapse in his ability to be clean.

It will take quite a long time for your puppy to become reliably housebroken. Until he is a year old, do not expect too much. Occasional lapses during the first year are to be expected, since your puppy is still a young animal. When they occur, go back to the original housebreaking program again. As your puppy matures, lapses will become less and less frequent.

Submissive Urination

Some puppies, especially females, are prone to leak urine when excited or stressed, or during encounters with high-ranking humans or dogs. They will sometimes produce a small puddle when being greeted or scolded, sometimes turning on their backs or sitting with one hind leg raised. This is a natural response designed to appease. It is their way of saying "look (or rather smell this!), I'm still little, please don't hurt me!"

If you shout or get angry when you see this happening, your puppy will do it more, in order to appease you more. The best response is to

ignore him and walk away until you get to a place where any leakage will not matter. If your puppy makes a habit of greeting people at the door in this way, keep a sheet of plastic and an old towel close by and maneuver him onto this before greeting him or allowing him to be greeted by visitors.

It will take time before your puppy is fully housebroken. Until he is one year old, do not expect too much.

Puppies that urinate will need to have their confidence built up. This will happen gradually as they get older, but try to avoid scolding or being angry with them. Show them what you want them to do instead. Such puppies are usually very eager to please and will do what you want as soon as they know what it is.

Chapter Eight

LEADING THE PACK

The Way of the Wolves

Wolves, the ancestors of our dogs, do not live in a democratic society. A strong hierarchical system exists in their packs. Privileges, such as the right to breed or choose the best place to sleep, go to the higher-ranking animals first. Once this order is established, there is rarely any need for infighting — most pack members know their places and are careful not to overstep them.

Young animals growing up in a pack learn where their own position lies during encounters with others. By the time they are young adults, they will know where they fit in because of the number of encounters they have won or lost. Some dogs seem to be natural leaders, whereas others are content to fill the supporting roles.

Depending on his breeding, his life in the litter, and how you treat him when he comes to live with you, your puppy will get an idea of how he fits into your family's pack. It is important that your puppy learns that his role is to be at the bottom of the pack right from the beginning, below all humans, young and old.

The Human Pack

Establishing yourselves as higher in rank than your puppy is one of the most important and kindest things you and your family can do for him as he grows into adolescence and adulthood.

A dog that sees itself as subordinate to humans will be much more acceptable than one that views itself as superior. It will be more willing to obey commands. A well-behaved, obedient, and compliant dog is a pleasure to own and is generally much happier than one in constant conflict with its owners' wishes. By firmly establishing your puppy's place at the bottom of the pack, you will be helping to ensure that he has a much better quality of life when he grows up, than a puppy that has been allowed to run riot. A dog whose behavior is acceptable is likely to be taken out and included in all aspects of his owners' lives.

In addition to having a dog that is better behaved, it is much easier to train a dog that views you as superior. Trying to train a dog, once he thinks *he* has the right to make decisions, is nearly impossible. If a dog feels subordinate to you, he will try to please you and will learn from you in much the same way as children will learn from a teacher who maintains a certain air of authority and who commands respect.

Life With a Dog Who is Pack Leader!

A dog that thinks *he* is pack leader will be making his own decisions. He will be out of your control, and will act like a spoiled child, trying all manner of tricks to get his own way. He will not obey commands or do anything he does not want to, and he will always want to be the center of attention. In our society, no one can afford to have a dog that is out of control, and life with a dog that thinks he is the boss is no joke!

If a dog is allowed to grow up with the idea that he is important in the human pack, he may begin challenging your authority as he begins to

It is essential that you are viewed as pack leader by your puppy. A dog that thinks he is leader will begin to control your life.

mature. (Bitches are no different from dogs in this respect.) His wishes will not always coincide with yours, and a dog that thinks he is superior may behave aggressively in order to "control" his humans.

Biting and other problems are common among pet dogs. They result from the dog being confused about its true position in the pack. Establishing yourself as pack-leader while your dog is still a puppy will prevent many problems later on. Trying to put an adult dog in his place when he already has ideas above his station is much more difficult, so begin now while you still have the upper hand.

Most dogs are not pack leader material but will fill a void if they perceive a lack of leadership in the household. Such dogs appear weighed down by the constant attempt to keep their pack under control and generally become much more puppylike and playful once the responsibility of pack leadership has been lifted from their shoulders.

When to Become Pack Leader

Establishing yourself as leader of the pack is much easier than you may think, especially if you begin while the puppy is still young. By the time a dog reaches adolescence at the age of about six months, he will already have assessed the members of his household and decided where he will fit in the hierarchy. Therefore, it is important to begin as soon as you collect your puppy and continue throughout his early life.

A Good Pack Leader

Being a pack leader is not just about being the boss and forcing your will on others. It is about taking responsibility, not only for decisions but also for sorting things out when they go wrong, for protecting the pack from harm, and ensuring that each member of the pack is comfortable and happy.

The key to being a good pack leader is understanding. Only when you understand your puppy will he respect and follow you without question.

The best pack leaders are usually benevolent and tolerant, but can be tough and uncompromising when they need to be. They will stand no nonsense, but are happy to be their dog's friend. A good pack leader knows when to stop and does not constantly bully the dog to force him to stay inferior.

How to Do It

In order to be a pack leader, a human needs to be viewed as superior in those aspects of life that a dog considers to be important. There are

certain areas and situations on which your puppy will place more significance than you. These are:
• Winning games and possession of toys.
• Sleeping places, territory, movement of the pack around the territory.
• Order of feeding.
• Attention and grooming from other pack members.
Dogs' lives revolve around things that may seem relatively unimportant to us. In order for us to be the pack leader, we need to look at each of these in turn and learn how to act like a top dog in each area.

Toys and Games – Playing to Win

In the wild, wolf cubs or wild dog puppies will play-fight among themselves and older members of the pack as they are growing up. During these contests, they learn about their own strengths and weaknesses relative to other pack members and, hence, where their natural position in the pack lies. In the same way, our puppies will play with us and learn similar lessons.

When playing tug-of-war, you should win more often than you lose. If you always win, your puppy will lose interest; if you always let him win, he will think he is stronger than you.

Strong-willed dogs (and people) play possessive games and play to win. Tug-of-war, which is a test of strength, is a favorite. If a puppy continually wins such games, he will assume that he is stronger than his owners, both physically and mentally. If your dog genuinely thinks that he is stronger than you, he will naturally assume that he is better suited to be the leader.

In this way, owners lose respect right from the outset, often unwittingly. Puppies are usually given their own set of toys as soon as they arrive home, and their owners rarely, if ever, attempt to reclaim them. Humans play games with their puppy using these toys, but the puppy always wins final possession of the toy when the bored human wanders off to do something else.

If you want to be a good pack leader, there are several rules that must be followed during games, especially those of tug-of-war. They are:

• All of the toys that *you* play with should be placed out of the puppy's reach. Give him toys that he can play with by himself but do not get involved in games with them. Play with him only with the toys that you keep in your possession.

A house-line (2-yard length of leash attached to the collar) can be extremely useful. Use it to help you recover toys from your puppy and to keep control.

• Invite your puppy to play with these toys often. Since you have the toys, it is your responsibility to remember to play.

• When playing tug-of-war games, win more often than you lose. If you always win, your puppy will rapidly lose interest in the game (no dog or human

enjoys games they are not very good at). If you always allow the puppy to win, he will assume that he is stronger than you. But if you win more often than you lose, your puppy will enjoy playing and you will be giving him the right message about his position in the pack. (See page 106 for ideas on how to remove the toy from his mouth without a struggle.)

Allowing him to win occasionally means having to let go of the toy at some point. If you have great difficulty in recovering the toy once you have let go of it, attach a house line to his collar before letting go. (A house line is a 2-yard length of cord; one end is fastened to his collar, the other end is left loose. Always remove the line before leaving your puppy alone.) If your puppy teases you with the toy, or runs and hides, pretend to ignore him, walk over to the end of the line, stand on it, pick up the line and pull him toward you to recover the toy.

Remember that puppies', mouths are full of teeth that are either about to fall out or are newly growing. For this reason, do not play too roughly. Let your puppy do most of the pulling. You are there to be the anchor and to make the game exciting by occasionally pulling gently on the toy. Do not hold the toy up high and wait until your puppy drops off as a means of getting the toy back, as this can damage his mouth.

Some puppies, which enjoy both chases and possessive games, will retrieve a ball for you several times and, when they are tired of chasing, will not let you have the ball back. Often they will tease you with it or try to entice you to chase them. A house-line can be used, as necessary, to allow you to win this game.

• Teach him to stop tugging on the toy and to let go immediately on command (see page 106).

• Play until you have had enough. (Try to stop before your puppy begins to get too bored.)

• Always stop playing instantly and put the toy away as soon as you feel your puppy's teeth touch your hands. He may have done it accidentally, but he will soon learn that being careless with his teeth brings an end to the game and will begin to avoid touching you with them. Stop playing also if your puppy begins to growl or if he is becoming overexcited. Always bear in mind what it will be like when he is an adult playing these games, and do not allow anything you will find unacceptable later.

• *Always* take the toy that you have been playing with away with you at the end of the game.

If your dog tries to play inappropriate games of tug-of-war with, for example, your sleeve, trouser leg, or the leashd, you will need to teach him that this is not acceptable. Make it clear that you do not approve, and prevent him from continuing by removing the object from his mouth before praising him calmly for ceasing to do it. Make sure that you apply these rules when you play games with appropriate toys. Later, once he has learned the command "to stop pulling and let go," you can use the command instead. Remember to praise him warmly as soon as he stops. If he is very excited, it may be easier to transfer his excitement onto playing with a toy, rather than trying to stop him from playing altogether. If he continues to play inappropriate games, despite being clearly shown that it is not acceptable, you may need to reduce the number of encounters that he wins and increase the number that you win. (See "How ambitious is *your* puppy?" on page 86).

Sleeping Places and Territory

In a pack of dogs, the dominant animals will choose the best place to sleep and rest. If a subordinate is in their selected place, it will move out of the way as the dominant dog approaches.

Dominant animals often like to get up high so that they can look down on the rest of the pack and survey the territory. It is the dominant animal that determines where to go and when. Since these things are important to dogs, allowing your puppy to sleep on (or in) your bed, allowing him on the furniture, and always allowing him through doorways or to run upstairs ahead of you, will give him the message that he holds an important position in your household.

To be a good leader, you need to control the territory and movements around it. This means doing the following:

• Make your bed a "no-go area" for your puppy from the start. Very pushy puppies should be kept out of bedrooms altogether, and it should be made clear that being allowed in them is a privilege and not a right. If your puppy jumps onto the bed at every opportunity or runs underneath and nips your feet as you go past, keep the bedroom doors closed and deny him access.

• Furniture should be for you, not your puppy, to sit on. If you make this a rule from the beginning, your puppy will never develop the habit of getting up there and will stay on the floor even when you go out. Encouraging him to get up there, allowing him to find out how comfortable it is, and then scolding him for trying to do so again is not fair. Always insist, quietly and calmly, that he stays on the floor. Remember to praise him when he does so. Get down there with him if you want to cuddle him, but do not invite him up.

• Doorways and entrances are very important to dogs, since they represent the beginning of another part of the territory. For this reason, if you both come to a doorway together, you must go through first and your puppy must follow. Do this by holding him back, by holding his collar as you go through or gently using your leg to keep him in position while you proceed. Teaching him to sit and wait involves too much effort, since you need to do this often, at internal doorways as well as external ones. Eventually it will become second nature for your dog to wait politely for you to pass through the door before he does. This is much better than having a dog that barges past you because he wants to go first.

Doorways represent territorial boundaries to dogs. Make sure you walk through doorways first. Eventually, it will become second nature for your puppy to wait politely while you pass.

This rule is especially important when your puppy is on the leash and about to be taken out for a walk. He will be excited and keen to get going. You will need to be quietly insistent that he follows you out. It is your way of impressing on him that *you* are leading the pack.

• If your puppy is lying in a doorway, do not step over him. Make him move out of the way instead.

• If you have a very pushy, willful puppy, you will need to impress on him that you own all the territory, and that if you want any part of it at any time, he has to move. Do this by occasionally removing him from

Food is an important resource to dogs; so it is best if a puppy is fed after his human family has finished their meal.

his bed or the place where he was lying, sitting, or standing for a few seconds. Do not let him back in until you decide to leave.

As you go up the stairs, make your dog walk behind you. Height advantage is important to dogs, and any situation where your dog gets up higher than you should be reversed, so that you can look down on him.

Order of Feeding

In a pack, it is the right of the dominant animals to eat first. The subordinates get what is left. This ensures that, in years of famine, the best animals survive to breed the next generation whereas the others die off.

To be a good pack leader, you should control the order of feeding. Try to arrange your puppy's eating habits so that he is given his main meals *after* he has seen his human family eating. This may not always be possible when your puppy is young because he will need many small meals. However, try to keep to this whenever possible, particularly when he grows up and needs just one or two meals a day.

Give your puppy just 15 minutes to eat his meal and then clear away any left over. Do not leave food down all day, since some very pushy puppies may view this as a statement of their importance.

Do not feed your puppy bits of food when you are eating. If you do, he may consider you to be a weaker animal because you have given up some of your food. Not feeding him when you are eating will also prevent him from getting into the unpleasant habit of dribbling and drooling over people who are eating. If you want to give him leftovers, make sure they are put into his bowl and given to him later.

Control over the order in which pack members eat is a small but important point. If feeding is one of the highlights of your puppy's day, it may be a very important point to him.

Attention, Praise, and Grooming

Do not always respond when your puppy demands attention. If you are doing something else, ignore him. He will soon realize that he can only get attention when you wish to give him some.

Dominant animals in a pack will seek and receive attention from their subordinates when they want it and will ignore advances from others should they not feel like company. Being aloof is a very superior way to behave.

To be a good leader, you will need to initiate most of the interactions between you and your puppy and not respond to all of his demands for attention. For example, when your puppy is lying down or has his mind on other things, call him over and make a fuss of him. When he comes to you for attention, do not always respond. If you are doing something else, ignore him by not looking at him, speaking to him, or touching him, but do not rebuke him. He will soon realize that he can get attention only when *you* wish to give him some.

If your puppy finds other ways to attract attention, such as standing between you and your visitors and barking, find a way, without speaking to him or looking at him, to isolate him from company with the minimum of fuss (use a house-line if necessary) so that his behavior brings about the opposite of what he wanted. Since he was trying to get your attention, shouting at him will provide just the reinforcement he wants and he will do it more. Consistently isolating him from company on these occasions will teach him that he cannot get attention when he demands it.

Your puppy also needs to learn to be groomed, touched, and restrained on your terms. Even short-coated puppies need to get used to this. See Chapter 12 for how to do this, and pay particular attention to between the hind legs (a very rude place for dogs to touch each other uninvited!) and behind the ears. Stop only when your puppy is standing still and accepting it. Then let him go and immediately reward him with his dinner or a walk.

Stealing

Stealing is another way of getting attention. Some puppies, particularly when they go through the adolescent stage, will play possessive games with their owners with objects they have found lying around. The owner sees the puppy with the object, which can be anything from a gold watch to a dirty sock, and gives chase. The puppy dashes from place to place and eventually lies down with his trophy, in an area where the owner cannot reach him.

To be a good pack leader, you need to win these "stealing" games. If you always win and your puppy always loses, he will find them unrewarding and will stop playing them.

Puppies will not steal when they are very young because they have not learned that it will get a reaction from you. Be sure, before you take action, that your puppy is doing this to tease you, not just because he was looking for something to chew. (If chewing is the intention, see Chapter 14.) If he is picking up items, looking at you, and teasing you with the object, you will need to win the challenge.

To do this, put down several items of no value to you and pick up all others so that you can react calmly when your puppy gets hold of something. For the next few days, whenever you are in the house with your puppy, attach a house line. When he picks up an article, walk calmly around him until you can step on the house-line. Pick it up, pull him toward you, and retrieve the article from his mouth. Say nothing, and give as little eye contact as possible. Then put the article back where it was and repeat until he gives up taking it.

Very soon you will find that your puppy has become bored with this game because he is not getting the reaction from you that he wanted.

Remove the house line, but put it back on for a few days if he regresses. Eventually, when he has matured, providing you have won all such contests, he will stop challenging you in this way.

Positions of Authority

When there is a conflict between two dogs, the higher-ranking one may demonstrate his superiority by placing his forepaws on the shoulders of the other and standing there for a moment.

In order to be a good pack leader, you should not allow your puppy to take up superior positions. These may be, for example, placing his paws on your shoulders while standing in your lap, or as he grows, putting his paws on your lap and staring down at you. Simply prevent this by standing up quickly whenever your dog tries to do this. Remain standing until the excitement dies down. Repeat if necessary (remove him from the chair if he tries to sit in it as you stand up).

Some small dogs like to jump onto the backs of chairs that you are sitting on. Remove them at once, using a house line if necessary.

Challenges and How to Cope

If your puppy is a true candidate for the top-dog position, he will be more intelligent than the average puppy and will find all sorts of ways to challenge your leadership. Providing you are aware of this and win any contests, you should find it relatively easy to maintain your pack-leader status. If you find that there are some situations in which he is behaving badly, think about how he may be winning during encounters, why you are losing, and why you are unable to stop him. Then work out a way to overcome the problem, so that the situation is reversed and you become the winner.

There may come a time, particularly during adolescence, when your puppy decides to test your authority. Some puppies never do this, but very strong-willed ones may, particularly those that have been given many privileges. React correctly, and it should happen just once.

Say, for example, that one day you find your puppy on the sofa, and as you approach to remove him, he gives a low, warning growl. You will need to react instantly and with enough force to let him know that he must never do such a thing again. Your voice is a powerful tool in such cases, and you should shout as loudly and frighteningly as possible while immediately removing him from the chair. There is no need to punish him physically, but your verbal aggression, body postures and facial expression must leave him in no doubt that his challenge was not a wise move. If you do this correctly, it should be a scary experience for your puppy so that he does not want to repeat the exercise. For this reason, you should be absolutely sure that your puppy is really challenging you before doing this. If in doubt, ignore him but keep a close eye out for similar behaviour later on.

Once the incident is over, do not hold a grudge. Forget it as a good pack leader should. But it may be wise to tighten up your pack leader procedures for a few weeks until your puppy is once again in no doubt about where he stands.

How Ambitious is *Your* Puppy?

All puppies are different. Both their genetic makeup and their early experiences will play a part in determining how ambitious they are. Some can be given all the privileges usually reserved for pack leaders and still not take advantage. Others will want to control the pack at all cost and exploit every opportunity to do so. If your puppy is naturally high ranking, you will need to win more games and challenges in order to stay in control. More submissive puppies can be allowed to get away with much more.

You will need to assess your puppy as he grows up and adjust his achievements accordingly. A submissive puppy can be made more confident by arranging for him to win more often, whereas a pushy puppy may need to lose many encounters with you if he is to respect you as a good pack leader. The important thing is to maintain a balance so that your puppy unquestioningly considers humans to be above him but not so high above him that his true character is inhibited.

As your puppy grows, notice how willing he is to put his paws and teeth on you and how responsive he is to your commands. These are good indications of how he views his position in the family hierarchy. If he is happy to jump all over you, chew and nip you, and rarely responds the first time to a command, you will need to review your methods of keeping him at the bottom of the pack. If he is more respectful, reluctant to put his teeth and paws on you, and is willing to please, but is still happy to play with you and enjoys your company, you have the balance about right.

Pack Leader Outside as Well as at Home

Being top dog at home does not necessarily mean that you will be the unquestioned leader outside. Establishing the hierarchy at home is of prime importance, but you may find that your puppy thinks he is better suited to leading the pack once you are out.

Having a dog under control outside the house is very important. If necessary, apply all the pack leader lessons when you are out on walks or when, particularly those concerning games with toys. Take toys out rather than allowing your dog to play with sticks, so that you stay in control of the games. If you find that your puppy is playing possession games that you cannot control because he can run away more easily, attach a line to his collar to give you more of a chance. Do not run after him, but walk around behind him slowly, until you can stand on the line and bring him to you. Try not to be drawn into chasing games that you can never win.

If your puppy thinks you are capable of leading the pack off your own territory as well as on home ground, he will be happy to accept second position at all times. Do not forget, however, that with leadership status comes responsibility, so it will be your job to sort things out if he is frightened by something or attacked by another dog.

Your Attitude

Your attitude is very important. If you think that your puppy should be given in to because you are the strong one and he is only little, your puppy will notice this weakness and take advantage of it.

Say, for example, that you meet someone in the street and stop to talk to them, but your puppy has just noticed a lamppost close by that he wants to investigate and he tries to pull you toward it. If you allow him to move you over there, he has just gotten his own way and you have lost a small contest. If, however, you make him sit and wait until you have finished talking, then allow him to go there as a reward for his good behavior, you have won the contest and increased your status in your puppy's eyes. Having the attitude that he *will* be reasonably well behaved without being so overpowering that he is afraid to be himself, will make all the difference.

Maintaining Top-Dog Status

Pack leadership is not a static state. In the wild, the old leader will be replaced by a stronger newcomer from time to time to ensure the pack remains fit. Similarly, if your dog notices that circumstances have changed and you are no longer the strong dog you used to be — for example, if you have recently moved to a new house and unwittingly allowed him more privileges than usual — he may seize the opportunity to move up the hierarchy.

Keeping to the guidelines offered here for the first 18 months of your puppy's life will help to establish you firmly as pack leader. This will give you a chance to assess how strong-willed your dog is, and you will then be in a good position to decide if he can have privileges or not.

If you have a strong personality and plenty of experience with dogs, you may be able to become pack leader without using any of the ideas here. However, most pet dog owners find it easier to establish and maintain authority, without resorting to punishment, if they follow these suggestions.

Everyone in the Family

It is important that your puppy grows up knowing that each member of his family is more important that he is. This means that children as well as adults have to keep to the guidelines, and they will need to be taught how to do this. If they cannot quite manage some of the stages, the adults will need to help out, particularly in cases where the puppy is large and the children small. Once the puppy has respect for all humans, young and old, he will have the right attitude toward other children and adults that he meets outside the home.

CHAPTER NINE

TOYS AND GAMES

How we play with our puppies is far more important than many people realize. This chapter will help to ensure that your puppy learns only good things from play sessions.

Why Play is so Important

Puppies that learn to play human games grow into dogs that view humans as a source of pleasure and enjoyment. Such dogs are much more fun to have around and are also more sociable. They probably have a better life in a human society than dogs that have learned to play only with other dogs.

Playing regularly with your puppy will help you form a strong bond.

Playing games is more than just a way for you and your puppy to have fun, although having fun during games is essential. Games allow the participants to find out about each other and learn about the character of the other player. Strengths and weaknesses are exposed, and the players' qualities and traits become apparent. Fear of the unknown lessens during play while the puppy and owner become more familiar with each other. New things are discovered as both seek ways to enhance the game, and a better understanding will develop between you and your puppy.

Playing regularly with a puppy develops a strong bond between you. It is possible to see a dog every day for years, and even be its only source of food, without developing a strong bond with it. Several play sessions, however, will help you to form an attachment and establish friendship and mutual trust. Being friends with your puppy is essential if he is to be trained easily and effectively. If he really wants to please you, and you are fun to be with, he will work harder to do as you ask. And of course, you will have more fun too.

The more games you play with your puppy, the more he will consider you to be the most interesting thing in his world. The more he wants to be with you and please you, the easier it will be to control him.

If your puppy stays near you on a walk, waiting for you to throw a toy, he will not wander off by himself and get into trouble. If he wants to chase the toy you are carrying, he will not find his own games by chasing cats, joggers, livestock, or a car. As you are so interesting, he is likely to rush back to you in case you are going to play a game with him, and he will not tear around with the other dogs in the park, making you late for work while you try to catch him.

Games are also an outlet for dogs' natural hunting abilities, many of which they still retain. Diverting your dog's instinctive desire to hunt, chase, and kill prey toward toys will prevent him from finding hunting outlets elsewhere. Some dogs, particularly those of the working breeds, are bred to be physically active and mentally alert all day. This is just not possible in most pet homes, and in the absence of any work to do, play is a useful substitute.

Adequate physical and mental exercise is essential, especially as your puppy matures and becomes a young adult. Lack of exercise can result in a bored, discontented dog with more energy than he knows what to do with. Very often, such excess energy is the cause of unwanted behaviors as the dog finds alternative outlets for it. Several strenuous play sessions, given at varying intervals throughout the day, can result in a dog that is well adjusted, contented, and looking forward to the next time you bring out the toys.

Since puppies, particularly those of the large, heavy breeds, should not be walked long distances until their bones have matured, play with toys provides a useful way to use up some of their exuberance.

Several short play sessions spread throughout the day are preferable to one long play session. Try to play with your puppy when he is being good — that is, not doing something you disapprove of. You will then be rewarding good behavior, and he will be more likely to do it next time. If you get the toys out only when he is becoming a nuisance, his general behavior will get worse.

Once your puppy knows just how much fun games with toys can be, you can use the toys themselves as a reward for a training exercise. Games with toys can also be used to your advantage in other areas — for example, overcoming your puppy's shyness with other people or any other fears that he may develop (see Chapter 10). Above all, toys are one of the most effective ways for you to establish and maintain a strong bond with your puppy.

Different Games for Different Dogs

A toy can be anything that is nontoxic and that won't splinter or cause harm in any way — for example, an old sock that has been stuffed with other old socks, or a piece of strong fur fabric. Toys should always be large enough not to be swallowed and should be eliminated before they break up into smaller pieces. Some puppies prefer soft things that they can bite onto initially, especially when teething, and will progress to harder, more solid toys later.

The various breeds of dog have been bred to serve different purposes, and since games are a substitute for the work they used to perform, different breeds will often prefer to play different types of games. There are basically three types of games:

• Chase and retrieve games — often preferred by herding dogs, gundogs, and hounds.

• Possession games (tug-of-war) — often preferred by guard dogs and bull breeds.

• "Shake and kill" games (squeaky-toy games) — often preferred by the terrier breeds.

Most puppies will play all games but will often prefer one type to the others. As your puppy begins to show a preference, it is advisable to buy toys that suit the type of game you are playing. It is, for example, much easier to play games of chase with balls and frisbees than to throw a knotted rope. Similarly, it is easier to remove a rubber toy from the mouth of a tug-of-war player than it is to try to fish out a ball.

An everchanging variety of toys will help to keep both you and your puppy interested. Puppies are no different from children in this respect and will appreciate a new toy or a different game occasionally. Since you are also a participant in the game, you will need to stay interested too. Sometimes buying a new toy, or rediscovering an old one, can improve games for you as well as your pet.

The purpose of play is to develop skills that may be useful later. Domestic dogs remain playful throughout their lives.

Some safe puppy toys.

Keep a toy in your coat pocket so that you always have one to play with when you're out on a walk. Playing with toys instead of sticks will prevent injuries to your puppy's mouth, eyes, or face. These often happen when one end of a stick becomes stuck in the ground, the puppy cannot stop in time, and runs into the other end. Simply ignore your puppy when he picks up a stick, and he will soon learn that it is more fun to play with the toys you are carrying.

Keep a toy in each room so that they are always available. You need only a short time to have a game, and if toys are readily available you can play whenever you have a few minutes to spare.

Games With Toys Versus Fighting Games

For all young animals, play is an important way of learning skills and strategies. Puppies learn a great deal while playing, so it is essential that they learn the right things. The games you teach, the rules that are applied, and the skills they learn during these games will affect how they behave later on.

For this reason, puppies should be taught how to play with toys rather than being allowed to continue with their natural game of play-biting. A puppy that is encouraged to play rough-and-tumble games with humans, to bite at our arms and legs, becomes well versed in these skills. Even dogs with good temperaments may bite in certain circumstances (for example, if they are injured in an accident and in great pain), and people are less likely to be bitten badly if the dog has no clear idea of how to go about it.

Skills that are learned in puppyhood are put into practice later on. If you do not want your dog to know how to bite humans, should he decide there is a need to do so, do not teach him how to do this now. He will call on what he learns in play should he need to react quickly in times of stress or excitement. Teaching him that there is no need to bite is important too (see Chapter 11) but if you do not want a dog that knows *how* to bite people, do not teach him; orient all of his biting behavior onto toys instead.

Good Manners During Games

Play-biting is the natural game for puppies. When he has settled down at your house, he will attempt to play with you in this way too. You will need to teach him how to play with you as he did with his littermates.

Have a toy ready whenever you choose to spend some time with him. As soon as you begin to stroke him or give him some attention, he will probably begin to chew on your hands. Make a fist with the hand he is chewing to make it more difficult to chew on, but keep it still and distract him at once by offering a toy instead. Make the game interesting by keeping the toy moving, wiggling it or rolling it along the ground in front of him. (If you throw it, he will have no idea of where it has gone, since young puppies have to learn this maneuver.) At first he may try to chew on your moving hands instead of the toy, but if you persevere he will soon learn that toys are much more fun.

Encouraging puppies to play with toys provides a good outlet for their physical and mental energies.

As your puppy learns to play games with toys, make it a rule that any unacceptable behavior results in an end to the game. Unacceptable behavior includes anything that will be unwanted as he becomes an adult. Think of him when he is full grown playing with a child. Would it be acceptable for him to growl at the child, even in play? Would the child be upset if your dog worked his way around the toy during a game of tug-of-war and bit his fingers to make them let go? Would it be all right if the dog came racing toward the child and tried to snatch the toy out of his hand?

Remember, anything you teach now will become your dog's normal behavior later on. Stop unacceptable behaviors by ending the game and walking away with the toy as soon as they occur. Your puppy will learn what causes the game to end and will begin to avoid those behaviors so that the game can continue.

Keeping Toys to Yourself

It is essential that your puppy has a variety of toys and chewable objects to play with and to amuse himself with at all times. Do not get involved in games with these toys but, instead, have another set of toys that are always kept in your possession. These toys will be more interesting to your puppy than those he has, and because he associates them with having fun with you, they will mean much more to him.

Teaching your puppy to retrieve is easy as long as you start before he has learned to avoid people when he has a toy.

Such toys can also be more delicate than those that are left with your puppy all the time. Squeaky toys, for example, can last longer if played with only when you are present; they would be chewed up quickly if left with a puppy going through a teething stage. Owners will often say their dog has no toys because as soon as they give him a new one he buries it, chews it to pieces, or hides it. By keeping them yourself, you and your puppy will always have toys to play with and the toys themselves stay novel, interesting, and safe.

Teaching the Puppy to Retrieve

Teaching your dog to retrieve is extremely useful because it allows you to get toys back easily and to stay in control of games. Playing "fetch" games is an easy way to exercise your puppy, and retrieving can form the basis of many other games that you can play with him.

When your puppy brings a toy to you, do not touch it, but make a big fuss of him. Touch him anywhere except the head region.

Teaching a puppy to retrieve is easy if you start early enough, before he has learned to avoid people once he has the toy. Begin by teasing the puppy with the toy and rolling it along the ground. As your puppy starts to run after it, give a command (e.g. "Fetch!") so he begins to associate this word with running out to pick things up. Once he has picked up the toy, use your voice to praise him and encourage him to come back to you. If you sound exciting enough, he will probably trot back to you carrying the toy in this mouth and wagging his tail. Keep your hands still so that he does not think you are waiting to take the toy from him, or he may try to avoid you and lie down with the toy elsewhere.

When he reaches you, do not touch the toy, but make a big fuss of him, touching him anywhere except around the head region. If you go straight for the toy, he will learn to avoid you and will eventually begin to stop coming back.

When he has had the toy for a few minutes (be patient!), he may drop it of his own accord or may settle down to chew it. Take hold of the toy and wait until he lets go. As he does so, give a command (e.g. "Drop it") and remove the toy. Praise him and throw the toy for him to chase again. As your puppy grows older and gets into the habit of coming back to you, you can begin to take the toy away sooner (See page 106 for how to get him to "leave" on command.)

Children and Games

Children and puppies usually play together happily, both getting a lot of fun from the experience and learning a lot in the process. However, puppies can just as easily learn the wrong ways as the right ones, and it is essential that an adult is present during play sessions to supervise the proceedings discreetly.

Remember that anything your puppy learns to do when young is the pattern for his future behavior. Children would not wish their puppy any harm, but they do not always realize the consequences of their actions. Observe the games your puppy plays with children. If he begins to play unsuitable games, either correct him or encourage the children to play a different game with him.

Keep Games Fun

Puppies are naturally playful, and it is not difficult to encourage them to play with you from the outset. The only exception may be a very shy puppy, which may need time and careful coaxing before he feels bold enough to attempt a game.

What *you* do during games will have a great effect on whether your puppy considers you to be an exciting playmate or not. Children are usually best at games, since they are often less inhibited than adults. Imitating their ways by squeaking, moving quickly, laughing, and being excited makes a puppy excited too. Be as silly as you like!

If you are a fairly reserved person, unused to being silly in public, practice in private. It will become second nature, and you will find yourself playing kooky games with your puppy in company as well. Onlookers will not think anything of it; everyone expects owners to be silly with their dogs, especially when they are puppies.

Movement excites puppies, so keep the toy moving erratically. Tying your puppy's toy to a piece of string and using it to make the toy "jump" may encourage a reluctant puppy or revive an old game. Be inventive and try new games whenever either of you begin to get bored with old ones. Make games fun for yourself too. Nothing motivates a puppy quite like our smiles and laughter.

Competition encourages some puppies to try harder to win the toy. If you throw a toy and allow your puppy to fetch it, he will enjoy the game of chase. However, if you throw the toy and sometimes race after it yourself, getting to it just before your puppy does and snatching it away before he gets to it, or sometimes allowing him to get to it first, he will make more of an effort the next time and will have more fun doing so. Teasing your puppy with the toy before you throw it will have a similar effect, but do not overdo this and do not encourage children to do it as they will often do it to excess.

Puppies will want to play games whenever they get excited about something. This could be anything, from your coming home to visitors arriving. During exciting times of day, you will often see dogs playing their favorite games. Labradors may bring you a slipper when you come home, Terriers may grab at and "kill" newspapers that have just been delivered, and some dogs may play tug-of-war with the leash during the initial excitement of getting ready for a walk.

You can use this natural tendency to encourage a reluctant puppy to play with you by getting out toys whenever he is excited about something. For example, keep a toy by the door and get it down to play with every time you arrive home. If you link all the exciting things of the day with the appearance of the toy, in the end the toy will become exciting to the puppy. Since dogs like to play their favorite game when they become excited, your puppy will eventually want to play with the toy whenever you produced it. This will have the additional advantage of preventing him from finding other, perhaps inappropriate, games to play during times of excitement.

At first, do not try to control the games too much or add too many rules. Nothing discourages a puppy from playing more than playing with someone who is bossy and always takes control. Do not insist on perfect retrieves, or a sit stay before the puppy is allowed to chase after the toy, until much later. Foster the enthusiasm for the games first, and put the controls in later.

Try not to get angry during games, which can sometimes happen if they are not going the way you intended. Stop the game and take time to think about what went wrong and how to prevent it next time, rather than confronting your puppy. Do not force yourself to play when you really do not feel like it or if you are overtired. If you become nasty during games, you will put your puppy off and teach him that you are not to be trusted. Always finish the games on a high note, before either you or your puppy have tired of it.

Games should be an entertainment and a recreation for both of you. If you can make all games fun, you and your puppy will have a great time, and the bond between you will grow stronger.

Other games to play

Once your puppy knows how to play with toys, there is no end to the games that you can teach him. A few are given here, but by being inventive you can modify these games or invent your own. As your puppy becomes "educated," the games you play can become more complex, which will be more interesting for both of you.

"Find It!"

The aim of this game is for your puppy to find a hidden toy by using his sense of smell. It is a really useful way to use up your puppy's mental energy before leaving him when you need to go out. It can be played either indoors or outdoors, and once they have learned how to play it, dogs seem to really enjoy it.

Begin by holding your puppy's collar and letting him watch as you throw a toy into long grass or roll it around a chair out of sight. Release him with an excited "Find it!" and go with him to do so. As soon as he finds the toy, praise him enthusiastically and encourage him to pick it up and carry it back to where you started.

Progress slowly and encourage him to find toys thrown into many different places out of sight. Then begin to cover his eyes when you throw the toy so that he cannot see where it lands. At first, try to make the toy land with a loud thump when it hits the ground so that the puppy knows it is out there somewhere.

Eventually you will be able to tell your puppy to "Find it" and he will know that there is a hidden toy somewhere close. Always praise the puppy and play with the toy whenever he finds it.

Fetch the Slipper

The aim of this game is for your puppy to retrieve a named article. It is another good way to use up mental energy. Although English is not your puppy's first language, he will nonetheless be able to learn words repeated clearly and often enough. Since he will be playing happily, he will soon learn the names of the articles you are sending him to fetch, and you can develop this game into something really useful, like fetching your slippers or newspaper from the other room.

Begin by throwing out two different articles — for example, a toy a and knotted sock. Allow your puppy to run after them and see which one he retrieves. Make a big fuss of him when he returns to you, and play a game with what he has retrieved. Recover the other object and throw both out again, this time telling him to "Fetch the — —" as he does so.

As he brings the correct object back, praise him well and repeat the name of that particular item again and again. If he brings the wrong object, take it from him without praising and send him for the other. Concentrate on the same object for several sessions until he is reliably bringing back the named object.

You will then need to teach him the name of another object in exactly the same way, using two items different from the first two. Once he knows the names of two objects, throw them both out together and ask

Playing games with your puppy is a good way to use up his mental energy and teach him to be useful.

him to retrieve each in turn. If he brings the wrong one, do not rebuke him but do not praise him either. Just quietly take the unwanted article, repeat the name of the object you want, and send him out for it. When he brings it back, fuss him and play a game with the object.

Repeated often enough, this game will enable you to teach your puppy the words for as many objects as you have the patience to teach, and it can be a good party trick for him to retrieve the correct item from a big pile of others.

Grown-Up Dog Games

Grown-up dogs are often taken by their owners to places where other dogs and owners meet to play competition games. These usually fall into four different categories.

Agility

Dogs learn to negotiate high jumps, long jumps, tunnels, hoops, high walks, and A-frames. Once they have learned each obstacle, this is done at speed, and dogs love it!

Obedience

Dogs learn to heel, come when called, retrieve a dumbbell, be sent away as directed, stay still when told, and retrieve a scented cloth from among unscented ones. It is a bit like dressage for horses, since precision is very important. If it is taught as a game it can be enjoyable for both dog and owner.

Working trials

This is the serious game that police dogs and their handlers often play because it involves many of the elements that make a dog useful to the police. Dogs learn to track and search for missing objects, as well as how to negotiate a 6-foot scale jump, 9-foot-long jump, walk at heel, retrieve a dumbbell, come when called, stay when told, and be sent away from the handler as directed.

Fly ball

This game involves teaching the dog to press a pedal on a box to make a ball fly out of the box, which he then catches and takes to the owner. There are usually a series of jumps in front of the box, which the dog negotiates on the way there and back. Once the dog has learned this, it

Agility (left)

Obedience (right)

Working trials (below)

is done at speed against other dogs doing the same thing. There is great excitement, and dogs love it!

Unfortunately for some dogs, some owners take all the fun out of these games by training too hard. Owners who keep the games light-hearted and enjoyable usually have more success and certainly have a lot more fun than those who must win at all costs.

These games are for grown-up dogs because most involve jumping, which is not good for growing limbs. Small obstacles that are very close to the ground can be practiced with older puppies, but it is really best to wait until they have matured physically before going any further. Other parts of these games can be taught at a very early age, but it should be remembered that these are just games and are meant to be enjoyed by both participants. Keep games fun, and you will have a dog that loves to work with you on any task you choose to set.

CHAPTER TEN

CONTROLLING
THE GAMES

If you want to have an adult dog that is always under control and obedient, even during times of stress and excitement, teaching your puppy some control during games is essential. Lessons and routines learned during games will be invaluable throughout everyday life as well as in a crisis. They become particularly important if you have acquired a puppy of a large or powerful breed.

Imagine your puppy as an adult, racing after a neighbor's cat or getting loose in a field of sheep. What chance do you have of calling him back if you cannot stop him when he is in full flight after a moving ball? If you cannot get him to drop a squeaky toy, how will you stop him when he is closing in fast on the pet hamster or he has just noticed the new baby makes almost the same noise as his toy? If you cannot make him let go instantly during a tug-of-war game, how will it look if he begins to play with the coat sleeve of a child who is screaming in fear and you have to go over and wrestle with him in order to get him off?

Teaching your dog some control commands during games will enable you to control him during times of excitement or in stressful situations. Being in

Your puppy should learn to wait while a tempting toy is thrown and not to go after it until he is given permission.

control of the games means you are in control of your dog. These control lessons should be taught only after enthusiasm for the games has been established. Do not expect miracles at first. Remember that your puppy is still a very young animal and it takes time to learn self-restraint.

Chase Games

Controlling chase games is particularly important if you have acquired a puppy from one of the hound or herding breeds, especially if he will grow to be large or powerful as an adult dog. Your puppy will need to learn two things:
1. To wait while a tempting moving toy is thrown and not go after it until he is given permission.
2. To come back when called, even though he is in full flight after his toy.

Waiting for Permission to Chase

Every so often during a play session, slip a short piece of line through your puppy's collar, hold both ends of the line, and tell him to "wait" before you throw the toy. He will attempt to move forward to chase the toy as you throw it, but will be prevented from doing so by the line holding his collar. Hold on if he struggles and wait until he is calmly accepting the restraint. Praise him and make a fuss of him for waiting. Then let go of one end of the line to release him, give your command to "fetch," and encourage him to retrieve the toy.

Every so often, reward him for staying with you by keeping hold of the line and dropping his favorite toy to him while you praise him and keep him in position beside you. If you keep him guessing as to whether he has to run out to get the toy or whether the toy is coming from you, he will learn to wait for you to decide what he should do.

When he is reliably waiting when you ask him to, you will no longer need to hold him, but be sure the command is firmly fixed in his mind and resume restraining him at any time if necessary. Remember that control reduces enthusiasm, so if you find that your puppy is becoming reluctant to run out, you could be overdoing this exercise and you will need to allow him to chase the toy right away more often.

Later, you can extend this exercise by making the object to be chased more interesting. Asking him not to chase a familiar toy rolling along the ground is one thing; asking him not to chase a rabbit he has just flushed out of long grass is another. However, it is possible to simulate this degree of excitement by offering your puppy a more exciting chase game. This will depend upon what motivates your puppy, but it could be achieved, perhaps, by exciting him and throwing a new or favorite toy a great distance, or by seeing that he wants to join in an exciting game with other dogs or children and asking him to wait as the dogs or children race by him before releasing him to play with them. Be inventive, watch your puppy, and you will soon find something exciting on which to practice before you encounter a real situation.

Elementary Chase Recall

This is a very useful exercise because most dogs, at some time in their lives, will be tempted to chase something they should not. Being able to call your dog back from a moving object is something few owners are able to do, but it is relatively simple to teach, especially if you begin with a young puppy. You will need to have a reliable retrieving habit before attempting this.

You will need two people and two toys. Begin by throwing a toy past your partner, who should be standing facing you some distance away. Do this several times, and allow your puppy to chase after the toy and bring it back to you.

About once in every 10 throws, at random, throw the toy toward your partner, who catches it and tucks it away out of sight. As your puppy begins to run after the toy, shout "Leave!" loudly. Since the toy he was chasing has effectively disappeared, he will eventually look back at you to see if you have it.

Elementary chase recall is an important exercise to learn; at some time in their lives, most dogs will be tempted to chase something they should not.

When this happens, tease him with the other toy and throw it in the opposite direction. Allow him to chase and retrieve this one, but try to make this chase more exciting, either by pretending to go after it yourself or by using a more interesting toy.

Eventually, your puppy will learn that when he hears the command "Leave!" there is no point in continuing with the chase because the more rewarding chase game is now back with you.

Since you are only stopping your puppy from running after the first ball once in every 10 throws, you will not be able to do much of this before your puppy is tired. Several sessions will ensure that he begins to get the message and he will become more reliable with practice. If you shout "Leave!" more than 1 time in every 10, he will start to hesitate before running out, which will reduce the effectiveness of the exercise.

Once you have a reliable chase recall, you will need to re-teach it in more exciting circumstances, as in the "Waiting for permission" exercise.

Use a tempting tidbit to teach your puppy to stop pulling on a toy on command.

Tug-of-War Games

Your puppy will need to learn to stop pulling and let go when asked, even during a really exciting match. It is helpful to have two tug-of-war toys for this: a favorite one and one less-favored. (See Chapter 8 for rules that should apply to all tug-of-war games.)

Begin by inviting your puppy to pull on the less-favored tug-of-war toy. After a few seconds, bring the toy in toward your body and keep it as still as possible.

Hold a tidbit in front of your puppy's nose. As

he begins to loosen his hold on the toy, give your command (such as "Drop!"). Lure him away slightly with the tidbit and reward him with lots of praise, the tidbit, and another exciting game with his favorite toy.

Practice this often, in small sessions, until he will reliably let go of the toy as soon as he hears the command "Drop!" Remember to reward him well whenever he does so. At first, teach this only when the game is unexciting — that is, you have only just begun to play and you are holding the toy quite still.

Gradually start to use the command during more exciting moments of the game, having first pulled the toy in toward you so that you can hold it as still as possible when you give the command. Work up gradually to giving the command at a time when your puppy is working very hard to get the toy from you. If he does not let go at once, go back to practicing at a less exciting point in the game and progress more slowly.

Your puppy will learn that when he hears the command "Drop!", the game he is currently playing becomes unexciting and that, if he lets go, he receives a tidbit and praise from you, together with a more exciting game with a different toy.

Shake-and-"Kill" Games

Never overexcite a puppy with games with squeaky toys. Do not replace "killed" toys too frequently, and if your puppy becomes obsessed with the game, replace the toy for a while with one that does not squeak.

Dogs that enjoy killing squeaky toys often have a predatory side to their natures that is easily excited. Since their behavior with squeaky toys represents what they are capable of, care should be taken when they are in the vicinity of young babies or small pets. Teaching some rules to this game will give you the control you need when necessary.
Your puppy will need to learn two things:
1. To come back when called, even when chasing the squeaky toy.
2. To stop "killing" the toy and to drop it at once.
The first can be taught using the elementary chase recall technique given on page 105, but use two squeaky toys instead. The second is easy to teach if you begin while the puppy is still young. Although it is not essential, it helps to have two squeaky toys, one of which is a favorite. Begin by teasing the puppy with the less favored toy and allow him to take it in his mouth while maintaining a firm grip on it yourself. Let him squeak it a few times and then hold a tidbit in front of your puppy's nose. When he smells the tidbit, he will probably leave the toy to try to take the tidbit. Give the command "Drop!" as he does so. He will eventually begin to associate this command with taking his mouth off of the toy. Lure him away from the toy slightly and reward him with much praise, the tidbit, and a really exciting game with his favorite squeaky toy.

*Your puppy will learn
that the command "Drop!"
means that if he drops the toy
he is playing with, he will be
rewarded.*

If he is more interested in the toy than the tidbit, hold the toy still but try to squeeze it until most of the air is out of it (and it no longer squeaks as your puppy bites it) before you try again. Since the toy has now become unexciting, your puppy should become more interested in the tidbit. If this is unsuccessful, try offering tastier, smellier tidbits or his favorite squeaky toy instead.

Practice this often, in short sessions, until your puppy is beginning to let go of the toy as soon as he hears the command "Drop!" in anticipation of getting the tidbit. When he is reliably doing this, try again without holding onto the toy. Have him close to you so that you can hold onto it as before if necessary. Eventually, you should be able to do this at a distance. Your puppy will leave the squeaky toy he is playing with when he hears you say "Drop!" because he is anticipating a tidbit, praise, and a more exciting game.

CHAPTER ELEVEN

PREVENTING BITING AND AGGRESSION

This chapter explains the main causes of aggression in dogs and suggests ways to proof your puppy against situations that may cause him to bite.

Puppies rarely bite in earnest until they reach the age of about seven months unless the provocation is extreme. Before they reach this age, they usually have little confidence in their own abilities and tend to rely on other strategies, such as running away or appeasement. As they mature, and as their confidence grows, they become more likely to resort to aggression to solve their problems. Owners are often unaware that such problems are developing until their puppy grows up and becomes aggressive.

By understanding why dogs bite and by removing the need for dogs to take matters into their own hands, owners can greatly reduce the chances that their puppy will grow up to be a biter.

Why Dogs Bite

Many people think that dogs bite just for the sake of it, but in fact dogs do not become seriously aggressive without good reason. Most canine aggression is simply the dog's only way out of a stressful situation. When he finds himself in a predicament that he cannot run from, he cannot sit you down and tell you what he is unhappy about or write a letter. The only means he has of expressing himself is with body signals. Too often, humans ignore these because they do not know how to read them. Should the situation worsen, the dog's only recourse is to use aggression to sort things out.

Many dogs will growl or bare their teeth as a warning before they bite. Unfortunately, owners usually scold the dog or become aggressive themselves when this happens instead of realizing that their dog is anxious, and doing something to reduce his distress. Once a dog has been taught not to growl or show its teeth in this way, it will often bite without warning, which can be very dangerous.

As well as a provocation, dogs need self-confidence in order to use aggression. This comes with age and experience. Strong-willed types usually have more confidence; naturally submissive types rarely resort to aggression. Dogs will have more confidence — and hence be more likely to resort to aggression if necessary — when on their own territory or if they are with other members of their pack (human or animal).

Whether confident or not, dogs do not resort to aggression lightly, and it often upsets them greatly, just as it upsets humans who have to resort to fighting. They do get better at it, however, and they will become very skilled at using aggression as a solution if stressful situations present themselves again and again.

The best way to prevent aggression is to proof your puppy against situations that cause dogs to be anxious, so that he learns to tolerate or even enjoy them. It is also important to watch for signs of fear through-out your dog's life, to heed warnings (i.e., body postures, growling, or baring of teeth) and to find a way to relieve the anxiety he is feeling during these times.

You need to understand why dogs bite and remove the reason that makes your puppy feel he has to be aggressive.

Aggression Toward Humans

Fear-induced aggression

Preventing aggression caused by fear is essential. Puppies should be socialized and protected from unpleasant experiences as much as possible.

Fear is the most common reason for dogs to bite strangers or people outside the immediate family. Dogs do not need to have had painful or frightening experiences with such people to become afraid. Undersocialized dogs are likely to be fearful simply because they did not meet enough people and have pleasant experiences with them while they were young.

While a puppy is young and shy, he will try to appease, hide behind his owner if he can, or run away from a frightening situation. As he matures, he will become more confident of his own ability to defend himself. In stressful situations from which he has learned there is no escape (for example, when on the leash), he may start to use aggression to try to make the threat go away. Once he finds out how effective this is, the aggressive displays often begin to get worse, until bites occur.

Members of the family who use force and punishment in an attempt to train a puppy are also likely to be viewed with mistrust, as are children who tease or torment puppies, and they are likely to be bitten during confrontations when the dog feels a need to defend itself.

Socialization and protection from unpleasant (painful or frightening) experiences is the key to preventing fear aggression. Do not force a puppy into a situation that he is obviously unhappy about. Allow him time to get brave enough to go forward and investigate, and try to make the experience a pleasurable one by using toys and tidbits. If he is restricted by the leash, or is backed into a corner, help him out by removing the source of his fear so that he does not learn to be aggressive in order to solve the problem. Remember that it is your responsibility, as pack leader, to protect pack members from harm and help them out of difficult situations, even if this means asking a well-meaning person who is trying to get your puppy's attention not to do so.

Ensure that all unavoidable upsets are countered with many happy experiences in the same situation. If dogs consider all humans, adults and children, to be a source of fun, treats, and games, they will not want to chase peple away with threatening displays of behavior. See Chapter 6 for ways in which to do this.

If you have a shy puppy, you will need to work harder than someone with an outgoing puppy. Your puppy should be sociable and friendly with everyone he meets before you can relax your socialization program a little.

Aggression toward children

This is usually fear induced. Children can appear very different from adults, and sometimes very frightening from a puppy's point of view. Good socialization with many ages and types of children is, again, the way to prevent problems.

Unfortunately, children often enjoy teasing dogs, and some can be unintentionally cruel. If your puppy has met and had many pleasant encounters with a wide variety of children, he is less likely to feel threatened by the occasional bad experience. A well-socialized dog will often feel competent to deal with a situation where he is tormented.

Territorial Aggression

Territorial aggression is a form of fear-induced aggression. On their own territory, dogs are much more confident about removing a potential threat than they are elsewhere.

If two wolves from neighboring territories meet, it is likely that the wolf on home ground will win the fight, even though he may be the smaller wolf. Being on home ground gives him a psychological advantage because the neighboring wolf knows he is not supposed to be there. The owner of a territory is also more motivated to defend the resources within it than the intruder.

However, a dog will attempt to get rid of visitors to a property only if he sees them as a threat. Adequate socialization will ensure that your puppy will be pleased to see visitors rather than want to chase them off.

Most dogs will guard their territory against intruders but socialization will ensure that your puppy will be pleased to see visitors, rather than want to chase them off.

This does not mean that he will not guard the house. Most dogs will bark when a visitor approaches, and most mature dogs will want to defend their property from people who are acting suspiciously, especially if you are not at home at the time.

Delivery people sometimes fall into this category from a dog's point of view, since they go away again as soon as they are barked at. Not only are they entering your dog's territory, where he is most confident, but there will probably have been many occasions where they have entered your premises, startled your dog into barking, and then gone away.

Although the delivery people were going to move on after they had made the delivery, the dog does not know this. To him, they do something unusual, such as rattling garbage cans or opening the mail box, and then run away as soon as he starts barking. If, one day, someone leaves the door open, the mailman may suddenly have a dog's teeth buried in his leg or his bottom as he goes back down the path. The dog is worried by the mailman's daily intrusion and is simply trying to tell him not to call again.

To prevent aggression to delivery people, take your puppy out to meet them often until he is mature (even if it means getting up very early in the morning!). Encourage them to offer tidbits and to throw a toy. Usually they are only too pleased to make friends with a puppy, especially if you explain why.

If necessary, a weatherproof box by your gate can be used to store food and toys, and delivery people can be encouraged to give these to your puppy occasionally as they make their deliveries. A few treats left at the gate with letters could encourage a puppy to be pleased to see the mailman at the door and to begin to look forward to their arrival rather than being worried enough to try to scare them away. Most delivery people are happy to do this rather than have to face an aggressive dog every morning, even if it is on the other side of a door. This will not prevent your puppy from alerting you when someone comes to the door when he is older, but it will stop him from growing up to be frightened of delivery people and aggressive toward them.

Small territories and ones with very definite boundaries allow easier defense from threat. This is one of the reasons why some dogs become aggressive in cars. This problem also has its origins in fear. The dog is not so much protecting the car as protecting himself. He has no means of escape and therefore needs to threaten intruders to keep them away and, since the car is a small and easily defended space, he feels confident about doing so.

Prevention lies again in good socialization. If your puppy has no fear of people, he will not feel threatened when they approach. For shy puppies it may be worthwhile asking people to go up to your puppy when he is in the car to offer tidbits and games so that he begins to see them as a source of pleasure rather than view them with mistrust.

Dominance Aggression Toward Humans

Dominance aggression is usually directed toward family members or people with whom the dog spends a lot of time. It is the most common reason why dogs bite their owners. Only ambitious dogs will bite for this reason, and before they do so they will have assessed the strength of the people they are challenging. If they consider them to be weaker than themselves, they will often bite during confrontations in an effort to stay in control. Prevention of dominance aggression lies in putting into practice all the procedures outlined in Chapter 8. Puppies brought up to know that their position is at the bottom of the pack will not challenge for leadership.

Excessive Play-Biting

Puppies will play-bite naturally and will need to be taught to orient their play onto toys instead, as explained in Chapter 9. However, some puppies play-bite more than others and some may not be so easily diverted onto toys.

First try the method outlined on page 93. If this is unsuccessful, keep your hand still and give a short, sharp shout in a loud, deep voice as if you have been hurt. (This will be most effective if you do not normally shout at your puppy.) Look at your hand and ignore your puppy for a moment. He will probably then start to wag his tail and attempt to lick your face. Praise him quietly and offer a game with a toy.

Repeat as necessary, but do not get into a cycle where you shout and your puppy gets excited and bites harder. If your first shout does not work, walk away instead and shout more loudly next time. Remember to praise him and offer a game with a toy whenever he stops biting.

If excessive play-biting is happening regularly at certain times of the day, try to anticipate the event that sets it off and restrain your puppy at these times so he cannot get to you. For example, if he becomes excited when the children come home and tears around nipping them, or begins to bite at you to attract your attention when you sit down to read, put him in his playpen beforehand so he cannot do this. Ensure he is receiving adequate play and stimulation at other times.

If your puppy continues to try to play-bite excessively, especially if it is designed to attract attention, review all your dominance procedures (see Chapter 8). Attaching a house-line to his collar whenever you are with him and using it to restrain him so he cannot get a reaction from you may discourage him. If not, an effective correction may be needed (see Chapter 18).

Puppies are also well known for having a "mad five minutes" every so often, during which they tuck their tail underneath them and tear around like a hound from hell. This is just a puppy way of letting off steam and is perfectly normal. What is not acceptable, however, is if

All puppies will play-bite, and they need to be taught to orient their play onto toys. Keep your hand still, make a fist, so it is not so easy to chew on, and wriggle a toy in front of him with your other hand.

your puppy rushes by family members during these times, biting them on the way past. If this happens, walk out of the room, leaving him on his own or, if it is easier, put him out of the room instead. This will help him to learn that such behavior does not bring him the attention he hoped for. If he continues to do it, reexamine your puppy's place in the family hierarchy and ensure that he is learning to play games with toys gently without growling or biting.

Most young puppies will also be stimulated to play by the sight of a pair of feet walking past them, especially if these are accompanied by a flapping skirt or trouser legs and particularly if they belong to exciting, playing children. Offered such a temptation, puppies will often run and attempt to wrestle with your ankles, just as they would have done if one of their littermates had run past them. Since this is painful and likely to damage clothes, it is unacceptable and will need to be stopped.

Providing you are playing enough games with your puppy at other times, you are entitled to make it perfectly clear to him that this behavior will not be tolerated. Stand still and tell him off loudly. Be scary enough to make him back off as he realizes his mistake. Then praise him for having stopped. Move away, and walk past him again later to check that he has learned what you intended. If he makes no move to follow, go back to him and praise him well.

Another way to tackle this problem is to put his playpen in a busy part of the house so that many people walk past it. Since he cannot get out of the pen, he will become accustomed to moving feet and learn that play only happens when people get toys out.

Food Aggression

Preventing food aggression is quick and easy to do if you start early enough. It is easier with puppies that were fed individually while still in the litter; puppies that had to fight over a communal bowl to get enough to eat may have already learned to guard their food.

Food aggression occurs because of a need to protect a vital resource. It is a natural and normal behavior pattern but one which can be, and should be, eliminated in a pet dog.

It is not a problem that is related to their position in the family hierarchy; a subordinate will often guard an item of food from a higher-ranking, stronger animal. A law of possession seems to apply. Dogs that have been hungry at some point in their lives are more prone to food guarding than ones that have always had enough to eat, because they have learned to protect the food they acquire.

To prevent food aggression, you need to teach your puppy that hands approaching a food dish are not coming to take food, but are instead bringing something more appetizing to eat. Once a puppy has learned this, he will welcome you rather than try to keep you away.

Never become aggressive yourself in response to food aggression, or you will teach your puppy to become much more aggressive next time in order to protect his food. Eventually this will cause a rapid escalation in the food aggression until your puppy becomes dangerous whenever he is eating.

Follow this procedure at mealtimes:

1. Call your puppy to you and place his dinner in a large bowl on the floor. Squat down beside him and, as he begins to eat, gently stroke and touch him all over, talking to him quietly. Begin on his back and side, progressing slowly toward his head. Stroke his ears and underneath his neck.

2. Take small pieces of food that are more appetizing than his ordinary food (for example, small pieces of chicken, liver and fat trimmings) and hold them in front of your puppy's nose as he is eating. Allow him to eat these tasty tidbits. Do this three times.

3. Prepare another piece, but this time hide it in the palm of your hand. Put this hand, palm up, in the center of his dish and as he begins to sniff at it, open up your fingers to allow him to find and eat the tidbit. Do this several times, sometimes digging around in his dinner bowl before offering the tidbits, and then leave him alone to finish the rest of his dinner in peace.

4. Try to do this every day until your puppy begins to wag his tail and look up from his bowl to see what else is being offered as you approach, then reduce it to just a few times a week until he is mature.

Protecting food is natural behavior for a dog. It can, and should, be prevented from escalating into aggression as your puppy matures.

5. When your puppy wags his tail as you approach, occasionally lift his bowl up, put a few tasty tidbits in the bowl and return it at once.

6. Once he is happy to let family members approach his food in this way, get other people to do it while your puppy is still small, especially children if there are none in your family.

Bones and Chews

The same procedure is required for bones and chews:

1. Give your puppy a bone or chew and allow time for him to gnaw on it.

Just as he is beginning to get bored with it, approach calmly and confidently, dangling a tasty piece of food from your fingers. Lure him away with this food and pick up the bone or chew as he moves away from it. Allow him to eat the tidbit and immediately return the bone or chew to him.

2. After a few repeats, he will begin to look up at you expectantly, wagging his tail, whenever you approach. You can then begin to offer him the tidbit with one hand while taking his bone or chew with the other.

3. Eventually you will be able to take his bone first and then open your other hand to reveal the treat. Always give the bone/chew back immediately, and he will

Teaching a puppy with a bone to accept being approached will prevent him from guarding and being protective of it later.

learn that you can be trusted and there is no need to guard his bone from you.

4. Ensure that everyone in the family can approach your puppy while he is gnawing a bone without provoking aggression. If you have children, supervise these sessions carefully until your puppy is happy to let them approach too. Always ensure that they have interesting, tasty tidbits to give and do not allow them to continually pester your puppy with this treatment. Teach them to respect other dogs with bones, because not all will have had the benefit of this experience.

Pain-Induced Aggression Toward Humans

Dogs will often bite if we approach them when they are pain. In trying to help them, we may have to cause them more pain temporarily, and they often bite in an attempt to make us stop.

Little can be done to prevent this, apart from trying to protect your puppy from illness and injury, as all good owners will seek to do anyway. Routine handling and grooming exercises will help to build a trust between you so that, if accidents do occur, your puppy is more likely to allow you to help.

Predatory or Chase Aggression

Predatory or chase aggression occurs when a dog finds an outlet for its desire to chase by running after unsuitable moving objects. The "prey" can be cats, sheep, ducks, horses, rabbits, or even small dogs. In the absence of "prey" animals, and without adequate opportunity to orient their desire to chase onto a toy, dogs may run after other fast-moving objects, such as joggers, cars, or people on bicycles. Dogs especially prone to this are those from the herding breeds or hounds, which are particularly stimulated by movement.

Usually the chase is enough in itself and the dog will pull up if the creature stops running. However, not many animals can be chased without becoming frightened, and this usually means that they try hard to evade capture, making the chase more exciting. If an inexperienced dog catches up with a fleeing creature, it will often pounce on it to stop it from running.

Once caught, frightened animals tend to become aggressive, and this only needs to happen a few times for the dog to learn to bite first as it catches up with its quarry to save itself from being attacked. Dogs will rapidly learn to nip the legs of joggers, attack little dogs in the park, worry sheep and horses, and attack cats in other people's yards.

Prevention involves socialization, control, and orienting your puppy's desire to chase onto toys (See Chapters 6, 9, and 10). Never give a puppy unsupervised access to prey animals by allowing him to stray or to wander far from you when out on a walk. Develop the chase recall (see page 105) so that should your puppy unexpectedly set off after something, you can call him back. Remember that dogs are often closer to their wild ancestors than we like to think, and they should never be left alone with small pets, such as hamsters, gerbils, or rabbits.

Aggression Toward Other Dogs

Fear-induced aggression

Aggression toward other dogs is often caused by fear. Inadequate socialization or bad experiences can cause a puppy to grow up fearful of encounters with other dogs.

As a puppy grows and matures, it begins to use aggression to keep other dogs away, particularly when it is on a leash because it will have learned that, once it is on the leash, there is no way it can escape. Such aggression directed at other dogs is usually made worse by owners who tighten the leash and become anxious themselves whenever they see another dog coming toward them.

Once they are off the leash, such dogs will often keep their distance from other dogs, although a few may want to be friendly. These will run up to other dogs, only to find that they are out of their depth and then resort to aggression to resolve the situation. To make matters worse, dogs that have been undersocialized often unwittingly send out the wrong signals because they have not learned to use their body language correctly. This causes some dogs to become aggressive toward them, which just aggravates the situation.

Socialization and protection from bad experiences is the key to preventing fear-induced aggression toward other dogs. If your puppy is attacked or frightened by another dog, ensure that he receives many enjoyable encounters with similar dogs in similar situations to overcome the unpleasant experience.

Dominance aggression toward other dogs

Some dogs will fight others because they have learned to play roughly as puppies. This applies particularly to puppies brought up with an older, tolerant dog that has allowed them to play rough games without correction. Puppies that learn to play rough games will continue to play that way as adults.

Few dogs will tolerate such behavior from a dog they do not know, and rough players will often be countered with aggression. A dog that plays too roughly rapidly becomes aggressive as he learns to bite first, before the other dog attacks him.

To prevent your puppy from turning into a dog that enjoys rough games, stop him from playing as soon as his games with other dogs begin to get out of hand. Do not let him do anything to a familiar dog that he would not get away with if he were doing it as an adult to another dog he has not met *Inadequate socialization or bad experiences can lead a dog to be frightened of meeting other dogs. This can lead to aggression.* before. This includes biting them hard, putting his paws on their back, and mounting them.

Always ensure that your puppy would rather play with you than with other dogs by reducing the amount of time he plays with them if necessary. Make sure that he can always be called away from a situation with another dog that appears to be getting serious.

Inter-Male Aggression

When male puppies become sexually mature, other unspayed male dogs may become aggressive toward them. This should not be too much of a problem if your puppy is well socialized, since he will know the body signals necessary to appease the other male. However, it will be more of a problem if you live in an area where several aggressive non-neutered males use the same small exercise areas.

Try not to worry too much about the odd aggressive incident; if you are anxious, your puppy will sense this and become anxious too. Instead, concentrate on playing with him when other dogs come into view so that his attention is fixed on you. Keep him on the leash and protect him from the unwelcome advances of other dogs by giving them a surreptitious squirt of cold water from a toy water pistol when they come too close.

CHAPTER TWELVE

HANDLING AND GROOMING

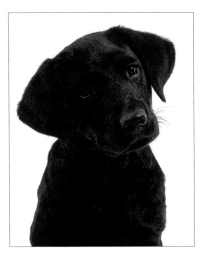

A new puppy must learn to enjoy being handled, held, and restrained by humans.

Humans are primates, and we like to touch, hold, and hug. Dogs rarely do this to each other and need to be taught to tolerate and enjoy it when humans do it to them. Even if you and your family do not intend to touch your puppy much, you will still need to prepare him for the times when children come running up and throw their arms around him or an adult, who should know better, pats him too heavily on the head.

The more puppies are familiarized with being held, handled, and restrained, the less they feel threatened by such experiences and the less likely they are to bite when touched, particularly during stressful situations, such as during an uncomfortable procedure at the vet's. Touching, holding, hugging and restraining your puppy builds a trust and an acceptance that will be projected onto people outside the immediate family.

Everyday Handling

Take every opportunity to handle and touch your puppy all over. When sitting down to stroke him, make a point of stroking him not just on the head and back, but everywhere (see pages 124 and 125).

Look in each ear and gently lift his lips to look at his teeth. It only takes a few minutes to do this, and if you do it every day your puppy will learn to accept it completely and even enjoy it as it will be a time when he has your undivided attention.

Most dogs need to have their nails cut periodically. How often depends on the shape of their feet and how much they walk on hard surfaces, but it is just as well to familiarize puppies with the procedure. Ask your vet to show you how to clip the puppy's nails when you take him in for his first vaccination. Ask him to show you the procedure even if the nails do

The handling exercises will ensure that your dog feels less fear and will be easier to handle when your vet needs to examine him.

not need cutting at that time so that you can accustom your puppy to it while he is still young.

Although handling sessions should be enjoyable, they should not have the atmosphere of a game. Your puppy will need to be taught to be sensible, and although care should be taken never to allow him to become fearful, neither should the sessions be fun, since you do not want your puppy to become excited. Happy acceptance of the situation is what you should be aiming for.

Handling exercises are a useful preparation for the day when something is wrong with your puppy. If he has almost eaten a fish hook and it is caught somewhere in his mouth, or he has something lodged at the back of his throat, he is much more likely to allow you or the vet to extract it if he is familiar with having his mouth opened. If he has hurt himself, he will be more willing to be examined if he trusts people and has no fear of being handled at other times.

When lifting or maneuvering your puppy during handling exercises, keep your hands flat. If they are not, your fingers will press into your puppy, causing discomfort, and he will try to wriggle away from you. Flat hands will mean that the pressure is evenly distributed, making the exercise more comfortable for your puppy.

RIGHT *Get your puppy used to being lifted up onto a table. Support his weight with a hand under his bottom and the other around his chest. Hold him firmly, but not tightly, and keep him close to your body rather than letting him dangle in midair.*

ABOVE *Lift his lips to look at the sides of his teeth. Open his mouth occasionally to look inside. Do this by gently prying his jaws apart. Open his mouth slightly and only briefly at first. Praise him afterward. As he becomes more familiar with this, it will become easier to do, and you will be able to open his mouth for longer periods.*

RIGHT INSET *Gently wipe around your puppy's eyes as if to remove any matter from the corners.*

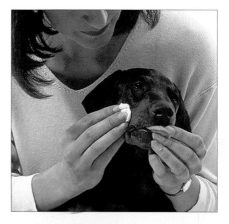

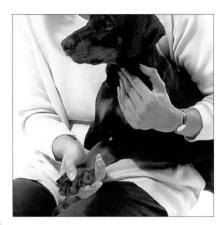

ABOVE *Pick up each paw, separate the toes, feel down his tail and down each leg. Talk to him quietly while you do it. Do not be bossy if he tries to pull away. (Puppies will instinctively pull their paws away when they feel them being held.) Repeat whatever it was he did not like, but do it more slowly and gently until he accepts it.*

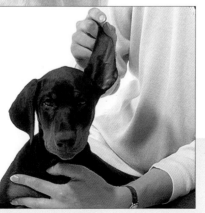

LEFT *Get him used to having his ear flaps held up while you look inside. Occasionally wipe the insides gently with moistened cotton balls. (Never put anything in the ear or poke around inside it.)*

Grooming

This is a more formal way to teach your puppy to accept being handled and restrained. Begin as soon as you get your puppy, and be sure to do this every day whatever the length of your puppy's coat. Use up some of his excess energy first with a short play session.

Start grooming your puppy with very short sessions — just enough to touch your puppy once all over. Progress to longer sessions gradually. When your puppy has stood still for a while and accepted what you are doing, break off suddenly and reward him with a walk, his dinner or a game. Once your puppy learns that standing still brings a reward, he will be more than happy to assist you by doing so.

Gently but firmly hold him with a hand around the front of his chest and shoulders. With a soft brush, begin along his back, down both sides, and then between the back hind legs and underneath his body. Brush each leg and then his head.

Occasionally put your puppy on a table to groom him. Follow the advice on page 125 for lifting. This will allow him to get used to the experience, which will be beneficial during visits to the vet or groomer. Make sure he does not fall off. If he tries to sit down when you want to brush underneath, gently lift him up into the standing position again. If he tries to bite at the brush, tuck a finger in his collar and gently turn his head back to face the front. If your puppy is very active and you find it difficult to brush him, clip a leash to his collar and tie this to a fixed object. This will give you both hands free, which will make things easier.

Be gentle near the head area, as it is very sensitive. If your puppy wriggles and squirms at any time, hold on firmly, using both hands if necessary, until he stops. Talk to him all the time in a quiet voice, praising him whenever he stands still.

Help your puppy to become used to people looming over him by making the exercise fun. He will then learn that this is normal human behavior and will not be afraid.

Looming and Grabbing

Although most owners know how to approach dogs correctly, some people will unwittingly try to touch a puppy in a frightening manner. They will, for example, loom over a puppy, staring straight at it and then bring down a hand on top of its head. Getting a puppy used to this will often happen naturally as part of the socialization process, but it is just as well to accustom your puppy against it just in case.

Try to make this exercise fun and part of everyday life. Occasionally loom over your puppy, extending a hand to pat him on the head. Then offer a tidbit and have a game with him. He will soon learn that this is normal human behavior and will cease to be worried by it.

In emergencies, people often need to grab at dogs, usually around the neck area, either for their own safety or that of others. If unfamiliar with this procedure, a dog may turn in self-defense and nip the hand that does this.

While your puppy is still small, proof him against this by gently grabbing him and offering him a tidbit as he turns to see what is happening. Gradually work up to grabbing him more vigorously, but never so that you hurt him. Always have a tidbit ready and make it into a game by

praising and playing with him afterward. The neck is particularly sensitive to being grabbed, as this is a place other dogs will often attack. Since it is also the place where most people will grab a dog, pay particular attention to desensitizing this area.

Puppies should get used to being handled by strangers. Supervise these sessions and be generous with the tidbits.

Handling by Other People

When your puppy is familiar with the handling and grooming procedures, ask other people to do them. Start with people your puppy knows well and is friendly with and work up to total strangers. Supervise constantly and help out if your puppy begins to look anxious. The generous use of tidbits during these exercises will ensure that your puppy learns not just to tolerate them, but also to enjoy them. It is also important that he gets used to being handled by children, so try to involve them too.

CHAPTER THIRTEEN

GOOD MANNERS

It is easier to create good habits than to cure bad ones. Good habits developed while your puppy is still young and impressionable will last a lifetime. Establish them by manipulating situations so that he finds it more rewarding to do the right thing than to do something you do not want. You can then reward good behavior, which increases the chances that it will occur again.

Bad habits are equally persistent, so it is as well to prevent them from happening. Behaviors you do not want, like jumping up, are often rewarding, so anticipate them and take steps to prevent them to ensure that your puppy never learns that they are worthwhile. This will give good habits a chance to become established.

It is wise to decide now what behavior is acceptable, foster this, and prevent him from doing things that you will not want him to do later.

Jumping Up

Never reward your puppy for jumping up or allow other people to do so. It is natural for a puppy to want to get closer to your face when greeting you and jumping up is his way of doing this. If you talk to him, look at him, or reward him with any attention when he does this, even if you scold him, he will learn that it is effective and will do it more often.

If you cannot greet the puppy right away — for example, if you have just entered the house and are carrying shopping bags — ignore him completely until it is convenient. Walk quickly past him, being careful not to step on him, until you are ready. If he is jumping up already, do not pay him attention, but instead turn away and walk a few paces so that his feet are on the ground before you bend down to greet him.

Since puppies are cute and cuddly, other people will want to greet your puppy too. They will quickly undo all your good work if they allow or even encourage jumping up. For this reason, always stay with your puppy when meeting new people and either prevent him from jumping up by holding his collar or teach the person how to greet puppies properly. Pay particular attention to how your puppy greets children. Children usually cause great excitement in a puppy, and they will be less likely to know what to do, so they can teach a puppy to jump up

very quickly. Supervise so that your puppy learns to treat them with respect.

Children in your family will need to know what to do if the puppy jumps up during play. Teach them to fold their arms, stand very still and look straight ahead rather than at the puppy while saying "Off!" loudly. Since they are now still, the puppy will lose interest in them and will wander away to find other entertainment. He will eventually begin to associate the "Off!" command with the end of his game and will eventually learn to respond to the word itself.

As soon as your puppy comes to greet you, crouch down and make a fuss of him. Stop him jumping up by keeping a finger in his collar and pulling down. Move him away if he tries to put his paws on you to climb up. Give him attention only when all four feet are on the ground.

Greeting People

This exercise will teach your puppy how to greet people politely. Begin with your puppy on the leash. Walk forward toward the person, or have them walk to you. Just before you meet, stop. Your puppy may attempt to jump up at the other person, but since you are holding him on the leash, he will be unable to do so. Your visitor should wait until all four of his feet are on the ground and any excitement has died down before asking him to sit. If your puppy does not sit immediately, ask your visitor to lure him into position with a tidbit (see Chapter 16 — do not attempt this exercise until you have practiced the sit often).

As soon as your puppy is sitting, the visitor should immediately come forward, crouch down, and reward the puppy with praise and a

There will be people or dogs you do not want your puppy to encounter, so you should teach him to walk past some of the people and dogs he meets rather than greeting them all.

tidbit. Hold on to his collar so that you can prevent him from jumping up if he attempts to do so. If your puppy gets up from the sit position, the visitor should withdraw his hands and ignore him completely. As soon as he has gone back into the sit, the visitor can then give attention again.

After a few repetitions, your puppy will begin to sit automatically when greeting people, although you will have to supervise meetings throughout his puppyhood just in case. Practice this particularly at the front door so that your puppy learns how to behave when visitors arrive. Arrange several sessions in which all the family go out through the back door and in through the front door, one at a time, ringing the doorbell and being invited in as if they were a visitor. The neighbors may think you crazy, but you will eventually have a dog that waits to be greeted rather than one who jumps up and sniffs visitors in embarrassing places.

Walking Past People and Other Dogs

All the socialization you are giving your puppy will make him pleased to see new people and dogs. However, there will be certain people and dogs that you do not want him to greet, such as people who are afraid of or simply do not like dogs, or a dog that may be aggressive.

You should therefore teach your puppy to walk past some of the people and dogs he meets rather than allowing him to greet them all. To do this, teach him to come back to you first before running to greet someone. Call him to you whenever you see a person or dog approaching and reward him well when he gets to you. You can then let him play with suitable people or dogs or keep him away from others. Eventually, he will learn the routine and will begin to return to you whenever he sees a person or a dog approaching. If you decide to keep him away from whoever is approaching, encourage him to concentrate on you by playing with a toy or offering a tidbit until you are past them. By doing this he will learn to walk with you past other people rather than straining and pulling to get to them because they are more interesting.

Excessive Barking

As puppies mature, they will begin guarding naturally at the age of about six to seven months. Owners who are unaware of this and who encourage their puppy to bark at a very early age end up with a dog that barks at the slightest opportunity. This soon becomes a nuisance and is difficult to control later.

Never encourage a puppy to bark. If you have done enough socialization, your puppy will be relaxed and happy and will not regard familiar noises and visitors as any type of threat. This does not mean he will ignore a serious threat to you or your home. Well-socialized adult dogs seem to know when to protect the pack or territory and will do so without being taught.

Never reward excited barking by giving your attention, talking to him, shouting, or touching him. It is natural for some dogs, particularly the smaller breeds, to bark when excited. If you encourage this when they are puppies, it gets worse as they get older. Look at the situation that prompted the barking.

Some dogs, especially small breeds, will bark when excited. Try to discourage this from the start because it will get worse as your dog gets older.

Say, for example, your puppy barks with excitement when he thinks he is about to go out for a walk. Make sure you do not reward this type of behavior by going on with the preparations for a walk while he is still making a noise. Instead, stand still, ignore him, and wait patiently, avoiding eye contact. Proceed with the walk only after he is quiet.

Keep your hand still when offering food to your puppy. Otherwise, he will learn to snatch at it.

Taking Food Gently

Puppies will quickly learn to snatch at food you are holding if you pull your hand away as they approach. For this reason, keep your hand still when you offer food so that your puppy can learn to judge where to aim his teeth. At first he will be clumsy and will probably try to chew your fingers as well, although he will not mean to. Try not to move your hand and he will soon learn to be more gentle.

If he has already learned to snatch at food, hold a tidbit between your thumb and finger but curl your hand round to make a fist before offering him the back of your hand. As he comes forward to snatch the food, he will bump against the back of your hand. He will hesitate and as he does so, uncurl your hand to present the food on your flat fingers. He will then take the tidbit without biting your fingers. Eventually, he will learn to come forward and wait close to your hand for you to open it and reveal the food.

Children should be taught this method of giving tidbits since their fingers are often more sensitive and they are more likely to pull their hands away, encouraging your puppy to snatch more hurriedly next time before the tidbit is taken away. Try to prevent situations where he will be able to snatch food from a young child who is wandering around eating. Either sit the children down or restrain your puppy until the food is eaten.

Never tease a puppy with food as he will learn to lunge for it, which could result in an unintentional bite.

No Begging

If you feed your puppy while you are eating or just afterwards, he will quickly learn to anticipate being fed at this time and will sit beside you drooling and dribbling. Preventing this behaviour is easy if you make it a rule of the house that no one is allowed to feed him at these times. Your puppy will then learn that he cannot have human food and will ignore humans when they eat.

Puppies also need to be kept away from the table while you are eating so they are not rewarded by bits of dropped food or those given on purpose by the children or visitors who may be tempted to do so. Teach your puppy to lie down by the side of table and praise him periodically for staying there. At first you may need to tie him or barricade him into this area until he has acquired the correct habit. Alternatively, you could use a baby gate to keep him out of the room where you are eating. He will then be able to see you while you eat and will get used to lying down and waiting patiently for you to finish.

Settle Down

Having a puppy that will settle down for short periods is useful when you do not want him involved in what you are doing, — for example, when you take him visiting at a friend's house or if visitors come to see you. Begin in your own house when your puppy is slightly older, is used to being restrained by a leash, and has learned the "down" command. Exercise him first to use up any excess energy.

Settle yourself comfortably with a quiet activity. Bring your puppy, on a leash, to your side and ask him to lie down. Lure him into the down position if necessary, and put your foot on the leash close to his collar. Praise him gently and relax. If he tries to get up, the leash will stop him from going very far, and he will soon lie down again. Praise him whenever he does so, but otherwise ignore him. Correct him if he chews the leash or your shoes and then praise him for lying quietly.

Begin with just a few minutes and gradually increase the time until your puppy can lie still for about half an hour while you do something else. When he is familiar with the exercise, teach him to settle down in situations away from home in other people's houses, on public transportation or anywhere your dog should learn to lie down peacefully.

Teaching your puppy to settle down for short periods will pay off when you do not want him involved with what you are doing.

Car Travel

A dog that accepts car travel as part of life can be taken anywhere and included in all aspects of his owners' lives. One that is constantly barking or rushing around wildly will be left behind.

Only on the very first journey home should your puppy be allowed to travel sitting on your lap. At this time, he has just left his mother and littermates and that is traumatic enough without having to adjust to a car as well. During all subsequent journeys, he should be placed at the back of the car in the position where you intend him to travel when he is older (and bigger).

As soon as your puppy has settled into your household, begin to accustom him to the car by placing him in it to sleep for half an hour daily. Cover the entire area with soft, absorbent material, put him in, and allow him to explore. Settle him in and close the door, being careful not to frighten him by slamming the door or tailgate too hard. Be sure he is sleepy and has had a chance to go to the toilet before doing so. The car should not be in the sun or in a place where people pass by.

When the puppy accepts the car as a place to settle down, begin to take him on very short journeys, sometimes with a walk in the middle as a reward. Negotiate corners and bumps carefully to avoid unsettling him. Remember that he cannot see out and so cannot predict what the floor he is sitting on will do next. If it is bouncing around wildly, he will become afraid of going in the car, which is the opposite of what you intend. When you reach home, take him straight to his toileting area before you both go inside.

Continue in this way, gradually increasing the distance, until he can accept quite long journeys. By doing this, you will gradually accustom him to car travel without frightening or exciting him. He will learn to view journeys in the car as nothing out of the ordinary and will patiently wait until you reach your destination.

Do not feed a dog before a car trip or he may be sick. Wait until after the journey when he has settled and is ready to eat again. Always give him the chance to go to the toilet before you take him out in the car.

Before you let your puppy out of the car, insist that he sit down for a minute or two after the door or tailgate is opened and praise him for doing so. Restrain him if necessary, because once he knows that car trips often end in a walk, he will be anxious to get out. If you do this at the end of each car journey while he is a puppy, you will have an adult dog that is under control when you open the car door, and sits politely waiting until you release him before he jumps out of the car.

CHAPTER FOURTEEN

CHEWING AND LEARNING TO BE LEFT ALONE

Teething

Teething occurs between the ages of 14 to 28 weeks (3½ to 7 months). During this time most puppies will have an uncontrollable urge to chew to relieve some of the discomfort and to facilitate the removal of puppy teeth and eruption of the adult set. Most owners expect puppies to chew at this time and usually provide their puppies with a good supply of things to gnaw on.

Exploratory Chewing

Just as the teething phase begins to pass, another more ferocious urge to chew occurs. This stage can last until a puppy is about 10 to 11 months of age. It tends to be more pronounced in the gundog breeds, particularly Labradors, perhaps because they were bred for their ability to use their mouths to carry things.

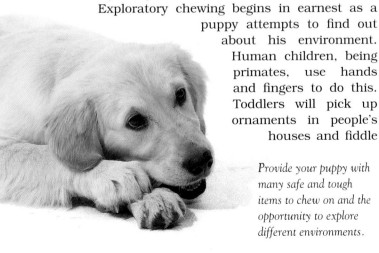

Exploratory chewing begins in earnest as a puppy attempts to find out about his environment. Human children, being primates, use hands and fingers to do this. Toddlers will pick up ornaments in people's houses and fiddle

Provide your puppy with many safe and tough items to chew on and the opportunity to explore different environments.

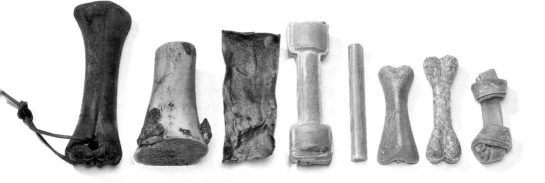

Safe chews: (from left) smoked bone, deep-fried marrow bone, basted sinew, and a selection of rawhide chews, and rasps.

with them in an order to find out about them. Puppies will make similar investigations but use their teeth and mouths instead.

Since puppies have no sense of value for objects, and they are now bigger, with stronger jaws than when they were teething, they can do a great deal of damage in a short time until this period has passed.

Providing your puppy with the opportunity to explore different environments will help this phase pass more easily. Puppies kept in one place tend to satisfy their desire to explore by chewing more items. It also helps to supply your puppy with several objects that are safe and tough enough to survive being chewed. These can be cardboard boxes, old plastic crates, and wooden logs, which puppies will clamber over, chew on, and explore. Replace and change these items frequently. Supervise your puppy while he has them, and remove any that become damaged and may be likely to cause harm.

Teaching Right From Wrong

In order to minimize the damage done by your puppy during these stages, it is important to deny him access to places where there are valuable or dangerous objects whenever you are not there to supervise him. The easiest, and ultimately cheapest, solution is to invest in a playpen, where he can go when you are not watching him (see pages 45 to 47). This can be filled with a variety of objects for him to explore and exercise his jaws on.

If you supervise your puppy's excursions into the rest of the house, you will then be able to teach him the difference between the right and wrong things to chew, and instill in him the correct habit right from the start.

First, provide your puppy with one or two chew toys that he has not seen for a while. Leave them out on the floor whenever your puppy is in the room. When you see him settle down to chew one, get down beside him and praise him well. Then allow him to chew without interruption.

If he ignores the chew toys and wanders away to chew something else, you will need to correct him in such a way that he thinks the correction seems to come from the object itself rather than from you. If you scold puppy when he begins to chew something he should not, he will learn not to chew such items when you are present. However, when you go out, he will not necessarily know that it is wrong to chew them. Dogs do not learn rules, they simply learn the consequences of their actions.

Instead, correction should appear to come from the object itself. If this happens, he will learn that it is unwise to put his teeth on that object and will be unlikely to chew it again even when left alone. To do this, keep a small water pistol at hand, or a plant sprayer adjusted to let out a jet of water rather than a spray. Just as he begins to chew something he should not, aim a short jet of water just behind his ear.

The intention is to startle him, not to hurt him in any way. His reaction should be one of surprise, and he should then wander away from this object to find something else to do. Hide the water pistol from view, look away, and if he looks at you, pretend you had nothing to do with the water jet.

The correction will be most effective if it happens just as he is about to chew on the object for the first time. If it occurs after he has been chewing for five minutes, it will be too late because he will already have been rewarded by his behavior. If you are too late, distract him by rushing out of the room calling excitedly, encouraging him to follow. Praise him when he comes and then watch him carefully, because he will probably go back to his new hobby, giving you a chance to correct him before he begins to chew again.

Your puppy should be taught not to chew on anything other than his chew toys.

139

Once he has gotten up and moved away from whatever it was he wanted to chew, go over to his chew toys and encourage him to come over to you for a game. Play a short game with him, using the chew toy, and when he settles down to chew, praise him and make a fuss of him.

In this way, your puppy will quickly learn that it is not wise to chew anything other than his chew toys. By providing him with a variety of chews, his desire to chew other items in the house will begin to diminish and he will get into the habit of chewing his things only.

Until he is reliable, never leave your puppy alone with the run of the house. If he chews something he should not, consider it your fault, not his, for trusting him too soon. There are bound to be accidents, just as in housebreaking, when you have a lapse in concentration. Do not shout or punish him. This will simply cause him to mistrust you. Just be more careful next time.

How long this process takes depends on your puppy and on how conscientious you are. Some puppies have a much stronger desire to chew than others and will take longer. However, no puppy should really be trusted completely until he is at least one year old and has gone through both stages of chewing.

When your puppy becomes an adult, his desire to chew will diminish, but it is important to continue to give him bones and chews throughout his life to exercise his jaws and to keep his teeth clean.

Learning to be Left Alone

Dogs are sociable animals and it is not natural for them to be isolated from others. A wolf separated from its pack will howl to try to locate pack members and will make valiant efforts to return to them. However, nearly all domestic dogs will have to be left alone at some time in their lives, so it is important that they learn to cope with solitude while they are still young.

If puppies are not taught to be left alone, great problems can be experienced when they are eventually left by themselves, even if the separation is for only a few minutes. Dogs that become anxious when left will chew, scratch at doors, dig at carpets, race around frantically, knock things off surfaces and windowsills, bark, howl, and perhaps lose bladder control. To prevent this, you need to get your puppy used to being left alone from an early age, especially if you normally spend a large proportion of the day with him.

Puppies, like all young, helpless animals, fear abandonment by their parent figure until they mature and become more self-reliant. Since you have become a substitute for their mother, you will need to teach your puppy gradually to be independent in a way similar to how it would happen naturally. Begin this process as soon as you get your puppy. Choose a time when he is tiring and is likely to settle down for a sleep.

Play with him a little beforehand and take him outside in case he needs to go to the toilet. Then put him in his bed and shut him in the room alone. Puppies will often feel safer if they have a denlike area to sleep in. Putting his bed under a table or into a recess, or in an indoor kennel with a blanket draped over it, may help a puppy to settle more quickly.

Ignore any whining, barking or scratching at the door. Sooner or later, he will accept being on his own and will settle down to sleep. While he is very young, open the door after he is asleep. He can then come to you when he wakes up and needs to go outside.

Repeat this exercise many times, gradually building up the time that your puppy spends on his own until he can cope easily with a few hours of separation. Teaching him to cope without you when you are somewhere in the house will help him to remain calm when he is left alone.

Never go in to a puppy that is making a fuss. If you do, you will be rewarding this behavior and he will do it more next time. Wait until your puppy is quiet before you enter, then go in and praise this behavior instead. Go in as soon as there is a quiet moment; leaving your puppy to cry for hours on end will only make him fearful of being left alone. Build up to longer absences gradually, but never faster than your puppy can cope with.

If your puppy has a very gentle and clinging nature, you will have to make more of an effort to teach him to be left alone than you would with a more independent puppy.

Never punish a dog when you return after an absence, no matter what has happened while you have been away. Your dog will not be able to link the punishment with what he did a long time ago, and it will not prevent him from doing it next time. He will think that you are angry simply because you have returned. This will cause him, to be anxious next time you leave him, since he will now be worried about your coming back, and this may cause separation problems later.

Learning to be left in the car

Even a small amount of chewing damage done by a dog left in a car can be expensive. Be careful during the chewing stages, and always leave a new and interesting chew toy for your puppy to concentrate on whenever you leave him. Accustom him gradually to being left in the car so he does not become anxious (see pages 114 and 136). Never leave a puppy or adult dog in a car on a sunny or warm day.

CHAPTER FIFTEEN

HOW PUPPIES LEARN

Trial and Error

Puppies, like us, learn by their successes and their failures. If a dog burns his nose on a fire, he learns not to do it again. If a dog barks for attention and everyone ignores him, he will eventually give up. But if he does something that is rewarded, such as raiding the trash can and finding food inside, he is likely to repeat it.

Repeating rewarding behavior or ceasing to do things that are unpleasant or unrewarding is the basis of any learning experience. This is just as true for humans and other animals as it is for dogs. In order to train our puppy, we simply make use of this process and manipulate situations so that he learns what we want him to do.

The Correct Relationship

Before you can begin training, you must have the right relationship with your puppy. He must view you as both a leader and a friend.

Successful training depends on being seen as important enough to issue commands. If your puppy looks on you as an equal — or worse, a weaker member of the pack — he will think you have no right to tell him what to do. By becoming a superior, what you want will become more important than what he wants. The higher your perceived status, the harder your puppy will try to please.

This high status should be achieved through everyday dealings with your puppy (see Chapter 8). You should not wait until the time comes for training to show him who is boss. Otherwise, a great deal of force is needed, which will make your puppy either resentful or apprehensive.

Another essential element for reward-based training is that the dog should see you as a friend. If he does, he will be relaxed in your company and there will be no apprehension to inhibit the learning process. Also, being your friend will make him want to please you because he appreciates your praise more when he does something right.

The old method of training involved a considerable amount of punishment, often administered by means of a choke-chain. Strong-willed trainers easily became pack leaders. This, combined with punishment for not getting it right, meant that the dog tried very hard to please. However, this method can be very unpleasant for the dog, which is why puppies were once left untrained until they were 6 months old. Before this age, puppies were too young to take the rigors of this method.

Motivation and Reward

All animals learn more quickly and retain more of what they have learned if they are not under stress. Therefore, teaching using only reward is far more effective and allows the puppy to put all his energies into learning the task in hand. An atmosphere of trust between puppy and trainer allows him to be more creative, and he is more likely to try new ways to obtain the reward, without fear of being wrong.

A reward can be anything that the puppy wants. The most obvious and easiest rewards to use are:

• Food

• Pleasant social contact with humans; verbal praise — most effective when delivered in a high-pitched, excited, squeaky voice; and physical praise (avoid patting the head — how would you like it?). Stroke the back or chest areas gently and lightly for most effect.

• Games with toys.

Different dogs are motivated by different things, and you will need to find out what is most reward-ing for your puppy.

Verbal and physical praise can be used as rewards when training your puppy. Avoid patting his head; instead, stroke the back or chest areas lightly.

Use small (¼ in cubes or less) tidbits as a reward when training so that your puppy does not become too full too quickly.

Reward-based training relies on the puppy wanting your rewards enough to put himself out in order to obtain them. Having a reward that produces sufficient motivation is important because the more motivated the puppy is, the harder he will try to learn a particular task.

Food rewards

If your puppy has just eaten and you are offering tidbits, he is not likely to work very hard to earn them. However, this does not mean that your puppy must be very hungry when you want to train him. In fact, being very hungry could actually disrupt the learning processes, as he may be able to think of little else other than obtaining the food. Just before a meal would be the ideal time, when your puppy will be peckish but not ravenous.

Your puppy will work best for tidbits that are smelly and tasty. Cooked liver that has been cut into small pieces and dried in the oven works well. If it is dried sufficiently, it can be stored in an airtight container so that you always have a ready supply to hand. Keeping several containers in different rooms of the house ensures that you are never far away from the rewards, should a few minutes of your time become available for a training session.

Whether you decide to use dried liver, one of the many dog treats on the market, or something else, make sure the pieces are small — about $\frac{1}{4}$ in^3 or less. Strangely enough, dogs seem to work harder if the pieces are small. They also become full less quickly, so that the training sessions can last longer.

After a few weeks of training sessions, you may find that your puppy loses interest in the tidbits that he used to work hard for. Just as we do, puppies can become bored with the same old thing, and changing the tidbits on a weekly basis will bring the response back up to expectations.

Pleasing You

Using food when training puppies makes it easier for them to understand what it is you want. Although they are rewarded by the food, a far greater reward is your approval. Puppies will learn much faster if you reward them, not only with food but with excited, happy praise and genuine approval whenever they do what is required. If you have the correct relationship with your puppy, trying to please you will be a greater motivation for him than working for food rewards alone.

Toys and Games

Later, when your puppy has learned the basic commands, you can use games with toys to motivate him to do as you ask. Games with toys are a continuation of your approval, and having fun with you in the form of a game is very rewarding for dogs, once they have learned how to play with toys (see Chapter 9).

Before you can teach your puppy something, his attention must be on you. You cannot teach anything if your puppy is looking the other way, walking away from you, or sniffing the floor around your feet. Before beginning a training session, play the Tail Wagging Game.

Tail wagging game

In a place where your puppy is not distracted by anything else and when he is looking elsewhere, go up quite close and say his name, quietly and clearly. As the puppy looks up at you, reward instantly with a small tidbit and lots of praise. Let him see that you have got another tidbit and hold it under your chin. Say his name, use your

Games with toys are very rewarding for dogs, once they have learned how to play with them.

145

voice to excite him and make his tail wag as much as you can. When he is at his most excited, give him the tidbit.

You could have a contest among family members to see who can make puppy's tail wag the most. Repeat often in many places or situations until your puppy will give you his undivided attention instantly whenever he hears his name.

You can then gradually begin to hold his attention for longer by quietly talking to him and maintaining eye contact before giving the praise. This helps to build his concentration time, which will make training easier, as will occasionally playing this game in more distracting circumstances.

Timing

Good timing is essential for effective training. Rewards need to be given as soon as the dog attempts to do the right thing, so that the required action is rewarded and encouraged. Immediate reward is best, but any time up to two seconds after the required action will do.

Rewarding too late brings confusion, since something else is being rewarded. Say, for example, you encourage your dog to go into the "sit" position and take one minute trying to get a food treat out from the bottom of your pocket. By the time you reward him, your dog will have mentally moved on to think about something else, perhaps getting up, even if he is still sitting, and it is this that you will be rewarding, rather than the act of sitting, which is what you intended to reward.

Good timing is not difficult but it is a skill that needs to be learned. Some people seem to have a natural ability, but they may have just had more chance to practice.

Playing the Training Game (the original idea for this type of game came from leading dolphin trainer Karen Prior, author of *Don't Shoot the Dog*) will allow you to practice this essential skill before attempting to train your puppy, thereby preventing your lack of skill from confusing him and getting you both off to a frustrating start.

The training game

You need at least two people. One person elects to be the "trainer," the other is the "dog." The trainer stays in the room and thinks up a task while the "dog" goes out until invited in (keep the task simple to begin with — for instance, the "dog" has to come in, sit on an appointed chair, and put his hands on his head).

The trainer has to help the dog to do the task without anyone speaking. The trainer is allowed to reward the dog with a blast on a whistle (clap hands if you do not have a whistle) whenever the dog progresses some way toward the desired goal — for example, if he takes a step in the right direction or produces a behavior that is something like the one required such as putting their hands up to their ears.

The dog will need to be as inventive as possible so that he can give the trainer something that he can reward.

The dog comes into the room and tries different movements to get a reward from the trainer. He will eventually be successful, and the reward from the trainer will ensure that the dog builds on this progress until the task is eventually completed.

Being both dog and trainer in this game is a useful experience. As the trainer you will find out how critical accurate timing is and how easy it is to accidentally reward an action that the dog will keep repeating because it was rewarded the first time. Do not blame the dog for this! Practice being the trainer until your reactions are sharper.

As a trainer or observer, you will also realize how long it takes to get the required action and how difficult it appears for the dog to understand what is required.

As the dog, you will find out how frustrating it is to work for a trainer whose timing is slightly off. Even if the timing is perfect, it will still be difficult to understand what the trainer requires. Finding out how taxing it is to be the dog, even if you have an experienced trainer, is a useful and humbling exercise.

As the dog, you will also realize how much pressure there is on you to do the right thing, particularly if there are a number of people in the room. Puppies feel that pressure, too, especially as they become more "educated" and realize that you want them to do something in particular, which they cannot immediately grasp. (This is why you will often see them sit down and scratch or yawn when they are feeling confused. They are engaging in displacement activity to relieve some of the tension they are feeling.)

By being the dog, you will also realize how tiring it is to have to concentrate on what is required — a good reason for keeping training sessions very short.

It is also useful to ask the dog what he has learned at the end of the game. Often, the dog will have picked up actions associated with the task that you did not intend him to learn. For example, you may have intended him to learn to come into the room, sit on a particular chair and put his hands on his head, but he may have learned instead to come into the room, walk toward the fireplace, turn round twice, then sit on the chair and put his hands on his head.

These unnecessary actions, which are beyond those required, are called "superstitious" behaviors, because the dog thinks that it needs them in order to get the reward. It is useful to realize how easy it is to teach dogs "superstitious" behaviors during training.

Teaching and learning without the benefit of a mutual language is not easy, but it is possible. By playing the Training Game, you will get to know how it feels to be your puppy and you will also learn or improve on skills that will help you to train your puppy. Reading about how to do it is not enough. To acquire the necessary skills, you *must* go away and play this game before you attempt training with a real puppy!

Keep Lessons Short

Learning is a tiring process, and young puppies have neither the stamina nor the powers of concentration for long training sessions. Keep lessons very short — about 1 to 3 minutes — but do lots of them throughout the day.

Is Your Puppy Enjoying Training?

How well your puppy learns will depend on how he is feeling. Dogs, like humans, learn best if they are feeling well and happy. Feeling off-color, frightened, or tired will inhibit the learning process.

For some puppies, an overabundance of physical energy can also have this effect, and giving them a chance to run and play before a training session can improve things.

Dogs learn more quickly if they are enjoying themselves, so keeping sessions fun will also speed up the process. Keep that tail wagging!

Body Postures and Words

The communication system of dogs is based on body postures rather than language (see Chapter 2). It is therefore reasonable to expect them to be better at learning from body and hand signals than from spoken words or sounds. This is indeed the case.

Long before they learn the meaning of each command, puppies will use our body postures and hand movements as visual clues to help them work out what it is we want. Therefore, to help them with the relatively difficult task of learning words, it makes sense to decide, not only on a simple series of spoken commands but also on a series of clearly defined hand signals.

The whole family will need to agree on this list and learn it, so that no conflicting signals will be given to cause confusion. Being consistent with the signals you use, both verbal and visual, will help your puppy to learn more quickly.

Initially, use both hand signals and verbal commands to teach your puppy. Later, as his understanding grows, you can begin to dispense with the hand signals and use spoken words only.

Puppy Training Commands and Signals

Action	Command	Hand/body signal
Give attention	....	....
Sit	....	....
Lie down	....	....
Stand up	....	....
Roll over	....	....
Walk on loose leash	....	....
Walk close	....	....
Come here	....	....
Stay	....	....
Go out	....	....
Don't do that	....	....
Good boy	....	....
Release command (e.g., go play)	....	....

All commands should be different and no two commands should sound similar. Avoid choosing commands that sound too much like the puppy's name — for example, Kit and "Sit." Make a copy of this list and pin it up in a prominent position where all the family can see it.

How Long Will it Take?

It takes regular training sessions over a period of about six weeks for one command to be learned reliably. Therefore, several sessions per day for a few months, at times of the day when your puppy is most responsive to learning, will soon establish the basic commands.

Aiming for Success

Throughout your training you should aim for situations where your dog gets things right first time and is rewarded for it. Do not allow situations to develop where you are repeating your commands and your puppy is confused or taking no notice. If you do this, you will rapidly desensitize him to the sound of your voice and he will learn to ignore you.

If you reach a point where you are not progressing, stop and think about why you cannot proceed. Plan your training sessions so that your puppy learns something, however small, every time and can be rewarded for it. If the new exercise is not going well, go back to something he knows how to do, so that you can praise him for it and end the session on a high note.

CHAPTER SIXTEEN

TRAINING
(PRACTICAL EXERCISES)

Dogs that respond to their owners and can be controlled by a single command or signal are much easier to live with. They probably have a better life as a result. Having to shout at your dog continually to get him to do what you want, or to physically restrain or maneuver him, is hard work and is probably not pleasant for the dog either.

The object of training is to provide your puppy with a set of commands that he understands, which can be used to make everyday life with him easier. A by-product of training is that you have a dog that is more in tune with you and begins to anticipate what you want so that he can be rewarded for it.

Using training methods that rely on reward for doing the right thing, rather than punishment for getting it wrong, enables you to teach a puppy at any age. Young puppies have a limited attention span, so keep their lessons short and simple at first. Training should be fun for you and your puppy; make training sessions informal and break off into a game at any time to keep learning exciting.

A Training Program

Work out a training program and set aside time each day until your puppy is at least 12 months old. Set achievable goals to keep yourself motivated. Remember to include all members of the family in the program, even young children (who will, of course, need supervision).

One of the best times to train is when you are out on a walk. Since you have set aside that time for your puppy anyway, it makes sense to use it to your best advantage. Short play/training sessions every now and then as you walk along will result in a well-trained, responsive puppy who is obedient outside as well as at home.

If you work hard on your training program for the first year of your puppy's life, you will have an adult dog that knows the basic commands and who will work well for you. All that will be needed will be a little extra occasional training to refresh his memory. Throughout the training, ignore any of your puppy's actions that you do not want and reward those you do. But do not scold your puppy for something wrong or he will be reluctant to try new things for fear of getting them wrong.

Coming When Called

Practice steps 1 to 4 on the following two pages. After about a week, you will not need someone to hold your puppy while you call him. Just wait until he is some distance away and thinking of something else, before calling him excitedly and doing the rest of the exercise.

Always have a reward ready for him when he comes to you. And always greet him enthusiastically and be really pleased with him when he reaches you.

Do this exercise only when you can be reasonably sure of success. If you call your puppy when he is far too excited about something else to respond — for example, greeting one of the family who has just come home — you will be teaching him to ignore you. In the early stages, never call him at such a moment. Wait until the excitement has subsided and he can be distracted before calling him.

He needs to get into the habit of coming immediately he hears his name. You should aim to call him back to you successfully as often as you can. Take every opportunity to call him when he would be coming to you anyway; for example, when he notices you have his dinner or when you return to him after being away.

You will need to be as enthusiastic about his coming to you each time as you were the first time he did it (make that tail wag). Once he has learned the command, reward only the more rapid and enthusiastic responses with tidbits or games (see Chapter 17). If this continues throughout his puppyhood, you will have a strong response by the time he is older.

When your puppy rushes to you instantly every time he hears his name and the command to come, you will be able to teach this exercise in more distracting circumstances (see Chapter 17).

Never spoil a good recall by punishing your dog for coming back. It is too late to be angry about whatever he has done. The important thing is that he did, eventually, come back. Punishing him when he returns will only make it less likely that he will come back next time.

Also, never call your puppy when you want to do something that he may not like, such as confining him or giving him a bath. Go and fetch him instead.

When on a walk, call your puppy back often, reward him well with tidbits, a game and praise for coming, and then let him go free again. It is important to do this during your walk, because otherwise you may be calling him back only at the end of the walk when you want to put the leash on to go home. Your puppy will learn that being called means the end of his freedom, and he may avoid you.

The object of this exercise is to make him want to come to you, not just for the tidbit, but because he wants to be with you. For this reason, it is important that you connect with him mentally and let him know how clever you think he is when he arrives.

1. *Ask someone to restrain your puppy and to release him as soon as you call. Begin by showing your puppy you have a tasty tidbit by holding it in front of his nose.*

2. *Run backward a few paces, stop, and call him to you, calling his name and your command several times in an exciting, encouraging way.*

3. Be "open" with your body language by holding your arms outstretched. As he begins to run toward you, praise him enthusiastically and continue to call him excitedly.

4. When he gets to you, hold the tidbit up under your chin, keep his attention for a few moments by smiling at him and praising him warmly for coming to you. Hold the tidbit out to him with one hand and take hold of his collar with the other while you feed him the tidbit. Keep hold of his collar until he has accepted the restraint, then praise him and allow him to wander away. Do not reach out to grab him. If you do, he will learn to avoid you. Do not put your hands all over his head, since he will probably not like this and will, again, learn to avoid you.

Walking on a Leash Without Pulling

While your puppy is still young and small, it is important that he learns that pulling on the leash means that he stops rather than goes forward. Most puppies learn the opposite of this, which is why so many dogs pull their owners down the street. Puppies that learn not to pull grow into dogs that are a joy to take out. Because of this, they are likely to be taken out more often and for longer walks.

Begin to practice steps 1 to 5 as soon as your puppy has become used to his collar and no longer minds it being around his neck or being restrained by it (see Chapter 5). Always use a flat buckle collar, never a choke-chain.

As your puppy gains experience in walking on the leash without pulling, begin to incorporate turns and obstacles. Warn him first that you are about to turn by getting his attention as you walk along and

1. Play a vigorous game with your puppy to use up any excess energy, then attach a leash to his collar and stand still. Encourage him to stand somewhere close to your left leg by luring him there with a tidbit. Praise him and feed him the tidbit when he gets there. (Professional dog handlers walk their dogs on the left, but there is no reason why you should not walk your puppy on the right. However, stick with the same side and make sure that all the family does so too.)

encouraging him to come close to you as you walk around an obstacle. Make it fun to be walking with you by praising him warmly every now and again.

Practice this exercise in the house and garden while your puppy is still unprotected by vaccinations and cannot go out for a walk. He should have learned to walk calmly beside you without pulling on the leash in these places before you begin to take him out for walks.

When your puppy goes out for his first walks, he will be excited by all the new smells and sights and will want to rush forward to investigate. However, it is important to instill good habits right away by never allowing him to pull on the leash. Be patient, and always allow enough time for walks at first. Progress will be slow to start with, but if you make a point of never allowing your puppy to pull on the leash, the teaching process will take less time overall. When you want to stand still — for example, to talk to someone — do not allow your puppy to pull you

2. Hold the leash in either hand and keep this hand pressed against your body so that the leash is a constant length. Adjust the length of the leash so that it is loose, but not so loose that it drags on the ground. Say your puppy's name to attract his attention, give your command for walking on a loose leash and move forward.

away from the place where you are standing. If you do, he will learn to pull into his collar in order to get to somewhere else. If he can never go anywhere by pulling against his collar, he will learn that it is pointless to do so and will give up.

If you have to go on walks during which you are concentrating on something else instead — for example, taking the children to school — it may be wise to find an alternative way to walk your puppy until he is trained. If he is small enough, you could carry him there and train him on the way home or put a halter on him while you cannot train him.

3. *Watch the leash. If it looks as though it is about to become tight, stop. (Hold the leash firmly against yourself so that it brings your puppy to an abrupt halt as you stop walking.)*

Allowing your puppy to pull on the leash during one walk and expecting him not to do the same on the next will confuse him and make it much harder to teach him to walk correctly.

3

4. *Encourage your puppy back into position and praise him. Wait until he is calmly waiting in that position before moving forward again. If your puppy goes around behind you or cuts across in front, stop and reposition him. Do not turn around as you do this — lure your puppy into position rather than moving yourself so that he learns to maneuver himself in relation to you. Repeat until he is walking beside you without pulling on the leash.*

5. *Talk happily to your puppy whenever he is walking beside you and stand still as soon as you see the leash about to tighten. This takes patience and time at first, but improvement will be seen after a few sessions. Do not be disheartened if you don't get perfect results the first time.*

Halters ensure you have control of your dog's head and that he cannot pull. Be careful to use the leash gently — it is easy to injure his neck by jerking or pulling on the leash too roughly.

1. *Hold a tidbit of food just in front of your puppy's nose.*

2. *Using the food as a lure, turn him until he is walking in the same direction as you.*

Walking to Heel

In addition to walking without pulling on the leash, it is useful to have another command that means "walk close and pay constant attention to me." This command can be used during times when you want to get your puppy past a distraction, such as another dog, or you want him to keep close to you while you negotiate an obstacle, such as a child in a stroller. This exercise is easier to teach with the dog off the leash.

Once your puppy has learned this exercise, gradually incorporate turns and obstacles. Always warn your puppy that you are about to turn by giving your command again before you do so. Once your puppy has learned to walk to heel, teach the exercise again in more distracting circumstances (see Chapter 17).

Continue this practice, gradually building up the time between tidbits. Eventually you will be able to keep the tidbits in your pocket and bring them out only occasionally. Keep in contact with your puppy whenever he is walking close to you and praise him enthusiastically to keep him with you.

Varying the speed at which you walk will keep this exercise interesting. Speeding up suddenly will be more exciting for your puppy, and you can do this if he is becoming bored. Try to make his tail wag all the time when he is doing this exercise.

3. *Praise him and give him a bit of food when he gets there.*

4. *Show the puppy that you have another tidbit in your left hand, but hold it up high enough so he cannot get it. Say your puppy's name and give your command for staying close. Show him with your body language that something other than normal walking on the leash is required. Usually this is done by straightening up, keeping your arms close to your body, maintaining eye contact and walking more briskly. Walk forward just a few paces, keeping his attention on you by talking to him excitedly. Feed the tidbit, praise him warmly, and stop. Before starting off again, show him that you have another tidbit. Never feed the tidbit if he has jumped up in an attempt to get it. Feed him only when he is walking nicely beside you.*

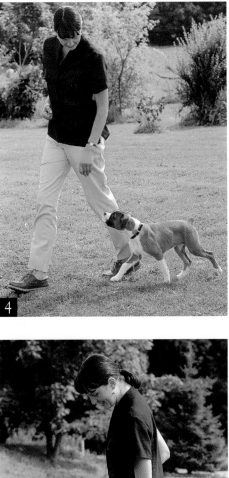

5. *If he begins to walk away from you, suddenly become very excited and enthusiastic so that he wants to be back with you. Finish the exercise only while he is walking well beside you.*

Positions: Sit, Down, Stand, and Roll Over

All these exercises can be taught in the same way. Lure the puppy into position with a tidbit, give the command as the puppy goes into position, and rewarded him as soon as the required position is reached.

Remember that your puppy will learn body language and hand signals before the spoken word. Keep these consistent throughout training and reduce them as response to your spoken commands improves.

Sit

Practice this exercise in short sessions, until both you and your puppy have mastered it and your puppy is sitting down each time you raise the tidbit above his head.

1. *While the puppy is standing, hold a tidbit just above his nose. As the puppy raises his nose to take the tidbit, move the tidbit up and back toward his tail, keeping it just above his nose all the time.*

2. *Hold the tidbit tightly between your thumb and forefinger so that he cannot get it until he is in the correct position.*

3. *As his nose and head move up and back, his bottom should automatically sink down toward the floor. If he jumps up with his forepaws off the floor, the tidbit is being held too high. If he backs up, the tidbit is being held too far back and too low, or you are moving it back too fast.*

4. *As soon as your puppy sits, feed the tidbit and praise enthusiastically. Stroke him gently and continue to praise him warmly as long as he stays in that position.*

When your puppy sits down as soon as the tidbit is held above his nose, incorporate the command "Sit." Say it obviously and clearly, just as your puppy's bottom sinks toward the floor. Remember to feed the tidbit and praise warmly while he is in the sit position as before.

During further sessions, keep the tidbit out of sight, say your puppy's name to get his attention and to get him looking at you, tell him to "sit" giving a clear hand signal, then bend down to lure him into position with the tidbit. After many repetitions, you will find that he will begin to learn the command and will begin to sit without being lured into position. When he does, feed the tidbit at once and praise enthusiastically.

Once your puppy knows the command, begin again by teaching him in different positions in relation to you (that is, teach him when he is standing in front of you, standing beside you, when you are sitting down or standing up). Teach him to sit on command from a lying-down position. Teach him in different places, and teach him with distractions going on around him.

If you have chosen "sit" as your command, be careful not to say "sit down" by accident, especially if you have chosen "down" for the lying down position. That could cause great confusion in your puppy.

Down

1. When your puppy is in the sit position, use a tidbit to lure his nose down slowly to floor level. Hold onto the tidbit if he tries to take it from between your fingers, and keep it in position.

2. With his head down, it is easier for him to lie down. Wait patiently for this to happen. If he stands up instead of lying down, lure him back into the sit position — do not let him take the tidbit — and try again.

3

3. *As soon as your puppy lies down, feed the tidbit and praise enthusiastically. Stroke him and continue to praise him warmly while he stays in position. When he lies down as soon as the tidbit is taken down between his paws, incorporate the command by saying "down," obviously and clearly, just as his elbows sink toward the floor. Feed the tidbit and praise warmly while the puppy is in the down position as before.*

Once your puppy has mastered this exercise, you can go on to further teaching sessions. Make sure your puppy is in the sit position, keep the tidbit out of sight, and say your puppy's name to get his attention and to get him looking at you. Tell him to lie "down," while giving a clear hand signal, then bend down to lure him into position with the tidbit. After many repetitions, you will find that he will begin to learn the command and to lie down without being lured into position. When he does, feed the tidbit at once and praise enthusiastically.

Once your puppy knows the command, begin again by teaching him in different positions in relation to you (teach him when he is sitting in front of you, sitting beside you, and when you are sitting down or standing up). Teach him to lie down on command from a standing position. Teach him in different places and also with distractions going on around him.

If you've chosen "down" as your command for this exercise, try not to use it at other times. For example, it is tempting to say "get down!" when your puppy jumps up or gets on the sofa. If you use it at these times, you will confuse him and weaken his response to the command.

1. *With your puppy in the sit position, put a tidbit just in front of him and, keeping it level with his nose, draw it slowly away.*

2. *If you move the tidbit away too fast, he may just sit still, waiting to be rewarded in that position. If this happens, move the tidbit back and go more slowly. If the tidbit is moving too fast when he gets up, he may walk forward.*

Stand

Do this exercise with your puppy and, for the following few days, begin to incorporate the command by saying "Stand," obviously and clearly, just as your puppy makes a move to get up. Remember to feed the tidbit and praise warmly while the puppy is in the stand position.

During further sessions, with your puppy sitting, keep the tidbit out of sight, say your puppy's name to get his attention, tell him to "stand" while giving a clear hand signal, then bend down to lure him into position with the tidbit. After many repetitions, you will find that he will begin to learn the command and will begin to get up without being lured into position. When he does, feed the tidbit at once and praise enthusiastically.

Once your puppy knows the command, begin again by teaching the puppy in different positions in relation to you (teach him when he is sitting in front of you, sitting beside you, and when you are sitting down or standing up). Teach him to stand on command from the down position. Teach him in different places and also with distractions going on around him.

3. *As he moves forward to follow the tidbit, he should automatically stand up.*

4. *As soon as he is on his feet, stop moving the tidbit forward, feed the tidbit, and praise him enthusiastically. Stroke him and continue to praise him warmly while he stays in the correct position.*

Roll Over

This exercise can be useful later on, when your dog is fully grown and the veterinarian needs to examine underneath him. Wrestling a dog to the ground so that you can look underneath him is much more difficult than simply teaching him to roll over.

1. *With your puppy in the down position on a carpet or mat, put a tidbit just in front of his nose and bring it around slowly toward his shoulder.*

2. *As the puppy turns his head to get the tidbit, his body should roll over to the side.*

3. *Be patient, because it takes time and perseverance for your puppy to get the hang of this.*

4. *As soon as your puppy is on his side, praise enthusiastically and feed him the tidbit. Stroke him and continue to praise him warmly while he stays in position.*

5. *Continue to do this for the next few days, gradually bringing the tidbit around further before rewarding him, so that, eventually, the puppy is rolling over onto his back.*

For the few days after your first session, incorporate the command by saying "Roll over," obviously and clearly, as your puppy begins to roll. Feed the tidbit and praise warmly while he is upside-down, as before.

During further sessions, with your puppy in the down position, keep the tidbit out of sight, say your puppy's name to get his attention and get him looking at you, tell him to "roll over," then bend down to lure him into position with the tidbit. After many repetitions, he will learn the command and begin to roll over without being lured into position. When he does, feed the tidbit and praise enthusiastically.

Once your puppy knows the command, begin teaching him in different positions in relation to you (that is, when he is standing in front of you, standing beside you, when you are sitting down, standing up, and so on). Teach him in different locations and also with distractions going on around him.

1. *Put your puppy on the leash, encourage him to go into the sit position, and praise. Give your command to stay, and stand beside him. Try to keep very still and relaxed at first, because any small movement may be seen by your puppy as a signal to move forward. Watch him closely for any slight movement that may indicate he is about to get up. As soon as you see a movement, repeat your "sit" command urgently and firmly, but not crossly. Praise him gently if he stays in position. If he gets up, hold his collar to prevent him from moving away and get him into the sit position again. If he lies down, reposition him at once. Tell him to stay, and make sure you stand still. Keep your puppy in position for a very short time (about 10 seconds) at first. Gradually, over a number of sessions, lengthen the time that your puppy stays in position by about 5 seconds each time.*

Stay

Practice steps 1 to 3. Always reward your puppy for staying in position with a tidbit, praise, and by stroking him gently (not so enthusiastically that he gets excited and gets up, though). Continue this only while he is in the sit position. Stop if he gets up, or you will be rewarding him for getting up. Give him a release command before walking away so that he will know when the exercise is over. Gradually build up this exercise until you can walk past and around your puppy while he stays in position. When you have a reliable "sit stay," repeat the exercise in a place where there are distractions. You will also need to teach the "down stay," which will be easy if you have a reliable "sit stay."

Never use this exercise to leave a dog without supervision in a potentially dangerous situation, such as outside a shop. He may get distracted and forget his training. For example, if he sees another family member on the other side of the road, he may run across.

2. *When your puppy can stay still beside you for five minutes without moving, repeat step 1, but take two paces sideways from him. Continue with this stage, for a number of sessions, until he can remain in position for up to five minutes, as before.*

3. *Once he stays reliably during the sideways movement, take two paces sideways and, watching your puppy carefully, step forward and in front of him. Correct him at once if you see him begin to move, and praise him when he settles back into the sit position. Retrace your steps to his side and praise him while he stays in position. Again, gradually build up the time he can remain in position until he is reliable for up to five minutes.*

169

Down at a Distance

This is a useful exercise to teach because it gives you some distance control, which may be useful in an emergency — for example, if your dog has wandered across to the other side of the road and there is no time to call him back before a car comes past. Obviously it is better to avoid such situations, but should they happen accidentally, being able to get your dog to lie down immediately may save his life.

Begin this exercise only when he has learned the "down" command and will lie down in front of you as soon as he hears the command.

1. *When your puppy is a pace or two away, give your command and hand signal for the "down" as you step toward him. Reward him enthusiastically as he responds.*

2. *After a few repetitions, as he begins to respond more promptly, lean rather than step toward him.*

3. *Eventually you will be able to stand up straight, give your command, and your puppy should lie down instantly a few paces away. Reward him well with a tidbit, praise, and a game if he responds correctly.*

4. *Gradually, over a number of sessions, increase the distance between you before giving your command. If at any time he does not seem to understand, go back a stage and repeat the exercise while he is closer to you. Teach him to lie down as he is running toward you in the same way. Begin when he has run almost to you. Gradually, over a number of sessions, stop him when he is farther and farther away.*

How to Teach a Trick

Teaching a trick is fun and a test of your ability to communicate with your puppy. A trick can be taught successfully only by using the reward method, so it is a good way to assess whether you are capable of teaching something without using compulsion. Tricks should be fun for both of you.

Make sure that the trick you choose is something that isn't demeaning or likely to cause injury. Choose something that can be useful, such as "speaking" on command, walking backward, or carrying a can of dog food. You will find it easier to teach the trick if you choose something that your dog will naturally be good at: terriers like to use their paws, gundogs like to retrieve, and herding dogs like to chase.

Tricks should be fun for both you and your puppy. Choose something he can learn that will be useful.

With all tricks, the secret is to break them down into small sections and then put them together to form a sequence. Always work on the last part of the trick first and work back to the beginning. This ensures that something familiar follows after each new section you teach.

For each small section, work out a way to position the reward so that your puppy can obtain it only when he has performed the action you require. Try to make it obvious to your puppy what he is required to do so that he gets it right first time.

Always reward the dog as soon as he does what you want. In the early stages of teaching each section, reward as soon as he attempts to do the right thing. Praise and give the tidbit at once (make that tail wag).

Do not ask for too much at once. Remember the Training Game and how disheartening it was when you did not receive reinforcement, despite trying several things you thought would be right.

Never get annoyed. If your puppy will not do what you want, think again; you have made it too difficult. Keep to two-minute sessions only, then stop and ask yourself what your puppy has learned. If the answer is nothing, think how to make things easier for him. Always allow a rest between each session. Practice each stage until, when you begin again, your puppy does the required action right the first time.

Once your puppy has learned the trick completely, remember to practice in different places and then with distractions. If your puppy seems to have forgotten all he has learned in a new place, start the training again from the beginning. He will learn much faster the second time, and faster still in your third new place.

Tricks are fun to teach, and because you are enjoying yourself, your puppy will have fun too. All training (for example, sit and stay) is really just a set of tricks: your dog is doing something that you want him to do in order to receive a reward and to please you. Keep all training sessions as lighthearted and as much fun as when teaching a trick, and your puppy will learn faster. Here are some ideas for future tricks:

- "Speak" on command
- "Quiet" on command
- Take an object and drop it in the trash can
- Carry your bag
- Carry his leash
- Weave through your legs as you walk
- Shut the door
- Fetch the newspaper
- Be a courier between members of the family (go to Dad, Mom, etc.).

Finding the Right Training Class

Attending a good training class is fun. It will help you learn, correct your mistakes, and stay motivated. However, it is important to find a class that uses methods similar to those given in this book. Some instructors still use a degree of compulsion and punishment. Avoid trainers who encourage the use of choke-chains, American or prong collars, or who do not advocate the use of tidbits and toys for reward. Attending a bad class will set your training back and may even spoil the relationship you have with your puppy.

Before signing up, go and watch for an evening without your puppy, even if the instructor tries to persuade you to take him. If you take your puppy, you'll be encouraged to join in and you won't concentrate on the methods they use. Watch adult dog classes as well as those for puppies. Avoid clubs that use harsh methods and make life difficult for the dogs or owners. If the trainers aren't using reward-based methods, don't join.

Avoid clubs where lessons do not seem to be under control or where there is a lot of chaos and confusion. It is becoming easier to find clubs with good instructors, and it is becoming easier as more instructors learn incentive-based methods. Ask your veterinarian to refer you to a class or professional association that uses such methods or write to the address given on page 190. You may have to shop around and be prepared to travel to find the right class for you. Dogs and owners should be having fun. If not, go elsewhere or train at home.

CHAPTER SEVENTEEN

DEVELOPING THE TRAINING

Dogs learn a whole set of associations surrounding an event, not just the one thing that you are trying to teach. Say, for example, you teach your puppy to sit on command while you are sitting on a chair in your living room. Your puppy will probably have picked up that:

a. if you are in a certain position in that room *and*

b. you are seated in a particular chair *and*

c. he is facing you *and*

d. you give the command in a particular tone of voice, he can get a reward for putting his bottom on the floor. He will not have learned the rule as literally "when my owner says 'sit!', if I put my bottom on the floor, I shall get a reward."

Take away any of these associations, and he may have difficulty in understanding what you want. So if, for example, you take him out to the kitchen, stand beside him, and ask him to sit, he will not know what you want him to do. This may be so even though he is more than willing to do something in order to get the reward.

You will need to remove all of the associations one by one (apart from the command itself) by teaching him the same exercise in many different locations, with him in many different positions in relation to you, using different tones of voice. That way, he will learn that it is the command itself which means that a reward is available for sitting. (For most pet dogs, this is the only command that they ever learn to obey, because it is the only one that owners repeat many times in many different situations.)

Practice each exercise in different places. Do not be surprised if, in the early stages, your puppy appears not to understand a command he is very familiar with at home. Simply explain what it is you want by patiently going through the teaching process again in the new situation, and he will soon learn to respond to your commands. Every time you do this, you will be adding to your puppy's understanding. He will take less time to work out what you want next time. Eventually, he will respond the first time wherever you happen to be.

(If you want to test whether your puppy really understands your voice command, get someone to hold his leash, turn your back on him, and give your commands. If he really knows the words, he will do as you ask. If he just stands there wagging his tail, he does not know them yet.)

You will need to teach your puppy the same commands, such as "sit," in many different locations, with him in different positions in relation to you, and using different tones of voice.

Learning With Distractions

Puppies need to learn that they must respond to you no matter what else is going on around them. A poorly trained dog will not listen to its owner's voice in distracting situations and will continue to think only of the distraction.

In order to have a dog that will respond to you even during the most interesting diversions, you need to reinforce his response to your commands steadily.

When you first begin to teach a new exercise, there should be no distractions, so that your puppy can concentrate on learning. Once he has learned, you can begin to bring in outside influences.

Start with small distractions that can be easily overcome. Keep your puppy on the leash so you have some control. If your puppy is not responding to you and is concentrating on the distraction instead, reduce the level of distraction or increase the amount of excitement you are generating. In this way, listening to you becomes more important. As he gets more responsive, raise the level of distraction slightly and repeat.

If you want to have a dog that will work with you at any time, you will need to proof him against all sorts of distractions. These can be children running and playing, other dogs going past, cats, joggers, or people eating. You should work with all of these situations if you want perfection. Making a list of all the areas where you will need control will help — for example, on walks, at the shops, near other animals, near water, near children's play areas, outside a school, in moving vehicles. The more situations you work through, the more likely it is that you will get a perfect response, despite what is going on in the dog's environment at the time.

Random Rewards

Once your dog has learned how to do something, there is no need to reward every response. Instead, offer rewards randomly instead of constantly. Reward only the better responses, and you will accentuate these rather than the weaker ones. At random, every now and again (about once in every 20 responses) offer a "jackpot" of praise, food, and games. Sometimes, especially if the response has been slow, offer no reward except a word or two of praise to let your dog know that he has done the correct thing.

You will find that, under this system, your dog will perform much better than if he were being rewarded every time, since he will hope that the next time he will get the jackpot. He is, in effect, gambling on the outcome — he is putting energy into a system where sometimes he may get nothing, but sometimes he may receive a huge reward.

This is the reason why people fishing sit all day on a riverbank waiting for the big fish, or people prefer to put money into a one-armed bandit than into a machine guaranteed to give goods in return. The system works for dogs too, and you can use it to good effect in your training.

Begin rewarding at random only after your puppy has fully understood what you want him to do. Randomly rewarding before he has learned an exercise will confuse him greatly, and it will take longer for him to learn.

Requests or Commands?

If your puppy has been brought up with the methods given in this book, he will have a good relationship with you, be happy to do as you say,

By following the methods in this book, your puppy will be happy to do what you ask and will want to please you.

and will want to please you. If your puppy has this attitude toward you, it is much easier and more pleasant for both of you to ask him to do things rather than to order him about.

Difficulties sometimes occur if your puppy has not been adequately proofed against distractions or if, during adolescence, he decides that he would rather do something else other than please you. In these cases you should change your request into a command, making it louder and more forceful and increasing the urgency in your voice. A strong command, given in a way that your puppy cannot fail to hear, will probably produce the response you want, especially since you have not desensitized him by using such a tone in everyday life.

If you are still ignored and you are sure that your puppy knows what you require, a short, sharp correction (see Chapter 18) will ensure that he takes you more seriously next time.

Becoming Educated

The more a puppy learns, the easier he will find it to learn more. As you work with your puppy, your training skills and his ability to understand your requests will improve. He will also learn that you want him to do "something" and will begin to try harder to find out what that is. If you progress far enough with his training, you will find that you reach an almost telepathic understanding as your puppy tries to anticipate what you want him to do.

CHAPTER EIGHTEEN

DISCIPLINE

At some point in their lives, most puppies have to learn that they risk unpleasant consequences if they continue to do something that a higher-ranking member of their pack has warned them not to do. Otherwise they will do whatever they choose, which will not always coincide with their owner's wishes. Since dogs must fit in with human lives, rather than vice versa, they need to learn that they cannot always get their own way.

"Natural" Discipline

A bitch will begin to discipline her puppies from the age of about three weeks. From this age onward she will begin to regulate their food supply by allowing them to suckle at certain times and not others. If they try to drink at an inappropriate time, she will growl at them, which causes them to move away.

As the puppies get older, some of the bolder ones will continue to try to drink even though she has warned them not to. This will result in an "attack," during which she will lunge toward the puppy, teeth bared, growling loudly and ferociously. The severity of this action will frighten the puppy, although it does not hurt him. The puppy will stop what he was doing and show submission in an attempt to appease his mother and stop any further hostility. This strategy works, and the bitch will then usually begin to wash the puppy and act as if nothing untoward had happened.

From this, the puppy rapidly learns not to ignore warning growls. The "punishment" is sudden, effective, and all over in a matter of seconds. Afterward there is no holding of grudges, and life continues as pleasantly as before. The only difference is that the puppy will have learned a valuable lesson.

When to Discipline Your Puppy

Only very rarely should you need to scold your puppy. Most of your interactions should be happy and pleasant. This will ensure that you become a good friend and your puppy will try hard to please you. At first he will be unaware of what he should and should not do. Every opportunity should be taken to manipulate situations so that he does the right thing and can be rewarded for doing it, rather than allowing him to do something you do not like and scolding him for it.

He will also be learning about his position in the family hierarchy. Once he has learned that his place lies below that of his humans, he will have respect for them and will want to do as they say. However, a companion dog is often allowed to get away with things that would not be allowed if he lived in a pack of dogs. For this reason it may be necessary to reinforce your position from time to time, especially during the adolescent phase, when the puppy is beginning to assert himself. Doing this correctly and effectively is important if you are to have an adult dog who is obedient in all situations.

There are two situations for which discipline may be needed. First, if your puppy does something totally unacceptable, it is better to correct this behavior immediately than to let your puppy be rewarded by it and, therefore, want to repeat it in the future. But save correction for behaviors that are completely unacceptable. For milder problems, it is better to restrain your puppy, teach an appropriate behavior and reward the puppy for doing the right thing instead.

Second, a bold puppy, especially during adolescence, may ignore your commands deliberately because he would rather do something else. Immediate correction will teach him that he must respond to you when you give him important commands. Before using correction in this situation, you must be absolutely sure that your puppy not only fully understands what to do but has also heard your command.

How to Do It

If discipline is needed, it should be given in a way similar to that in which a bitch will discipline her pups. It should be immediate, startling, effective, and should be over in seconds. Since the situation in which you discipline your puppy will often be more complex than that of the bitch with pups, your correction should be immediately followed by showing your pet the behavior you want him to display and rewarding him when he achieves it.

If your puppy is about to do something unacceptable, warn him before doing anything else. Do this by saying "No!", "Aaah" or something similar in a deep, stern voice. Puppies instinctively respond to the sound of a growl, and if your correction is comparable, your puppy will realize that you are issuing a warning.

If he is bold enough to continue with what he planned anyway, you will need to follow up your warning immediately with a correction. Try to give your correction before your puppy carries out the unwanted

*If your puppy does some-
thing unacceptable (left),
correct him immediately.*

*When he responds, praise
him (below).*

behavior, because it will be more effective at this time than if he is already absorbed in doing something you disapprove of.

The effectiveness of a correction lies in the element of surprise. You will need to get as close to your puppy as quickly as you can, preferably without his realizing it. You will then need to shout with enough decibels to startle your puppy and prevent his intended behavior. Continue to scold him for a few moments while staring at him and towering over him. With some puppies, especially if you have not surprised them, you may need to prevent them from carrying out the unwanted behavior while you scold them.

After an effective correction, your puppy's attention will be riveted on you. It is important that you use this time to show him the required behavior in this situation and praise him for doing the right thing. In order to do this you will need to revert to being calm and pleasant so that your puppy is no longer worried by you and can concentrate on what your require. This will allow him to learn that it was the particular behavior that made you act in such a way and he will be less likely to do it next time.

Any correction should be immediate and sudden. Do not build it up slowly or you will lose the element of surprise and you will have to be much more ferocious the next time. It is possible to desensitize your puppy to correction by building it up slowly. Give one warning, and if this is not heeded, give an effective correction at once.

If it is obvious that your puppy has ignored a command he has heard and it is one that you know he understands, it is necessary to give a correction to ensure that you will be obeyed next time. Never issue a command that you cannot enforce. If an older puppy has deliberately ignored a command, give a correction as suggested above. Then, while you have his full attention, give the command again and, when he responds, give as much praise and reward as usual.

It is important that your puppy learns that it is the unwanted behavior that annoys you, but as soon as he does as you ask, your attitude changes and you become pleasant again. Next time, he will want to do as you say because there is a clear distinction between right and wrong. Otherwise, if you continue to scold him, even when he is doing the right thing, he may as well continue to do the "wrong" behavior, which is rewarding in itself since he is going to be told off anyway.

Never use any correction while training your puppy. Ignore any mistakes he may make while attempting the exercises and reward the behaviors you do want instead.

Amount of Correction Needed

All puppies are different and they all have different levels of sensitivity. For some puppies, a slightly raised voice is enough, whereas with others, more is needed to let them know they are wrong. A correction that may seem mild to a bold puppy may feel like the end of the world to one that is more sensitive.

Tailoring your correction to your particular puppy is important if you want to avoid over- or under-correcting him. Watch the effect your correction has on him. If, after a correction, your puppy appears sulky and a bit wary of you, you are over-correcting. If your puppy continues to do things you have previously corrected him for, you are under-correcting him. If he stops doing whatever it is you do not approve of after one or two corrections, you have the level about right.

Environmental Correction

Another way to correct a puppy is to make it seem as if the unwanted behavior itself is causing the correction. When your puppy is about to do something unacceptable, a small fright should be enough to convince him that this is not a wise course of action. The best way to achieve this is to aim a short squirt of water from a water pistol just behind his ear or set up a booby trap so that unwanted actions bring about a startling reaction. The fright should be of a level that causes the puppy to stop the behavior and wander away to find something else to do. Too little fright, and the behavior will continue. Too much, and you will have caused unnecessary anxiety to your puppy.

Timing is important. The correction should come just as the puppy is about to begin the unwanted behavior. If he has already started, he will be rewarded by his actions and the correction may not be sufficient. If the behavior has already begun, distract him from it and try again later.

Environmental correction is useful in cases where you do not want to be connected with the behavior in question. Say, for example, your puppy has grown large enough to jump up and take food off the table. If you see him and scold him, he will learn that this action gets him into trouble only when you are in the room but that it is rewarding to do it when you are not there. Environmental correction will allow you to teach him that taking food off the table is not wise, no matter who is present at the time.

Why Physical Punishment Does Not Work

It is not necessary or desirable to use physical punishment to bring up a well-adjusted, well-mannered dog. Not only is it unnecessary, but it is very unpleasant for the puppy, and an excess of it can cause resentment and fear of the owners and a mistrust of humans in general. It will weaken the bond between you and your puppy and spoil any friendship and trust between you.

Physically punishing your puppy may also have an effect on his future character. Families who have used physical punishment to discipline their dogs often end up with aggressive dogs. Dogs that come from a family where no aggression has been used to raise them are rarely aggressive themselves.

If hands are used to administer punishment, the puppy may learn to be hand-shy. Later, if he sees a hand coming toward him — for example, if a child reaches out to pat him on the head — he may bite in self-defense. If the puppy learns that human hands never hurt and that they sometimes bring rewards, there will be no need for him to bite hands that are reaching toward him.

Unfortunately, physical punishment seems to be the first resort for humans when things go wrong. It is much easier to punish than to think first. Sadly, punishment sometimes appears to work well and to work very quickly, thereby encouraging owners to apply it more often. It appears to work so well because the symptoms of the problem are being treated, rather than the root cause.

For example, take the dog that is afraid of strangers because of a lack of socialization and that growls whenever they approach. If his owner applies sufficient punishment whenever this happens, the dog soon learns not to growl because he becomes too afraid of the consequences. The owner will think his treatment has worked and will recommend it to his friends. However, the real cause of the problem, the fear of strangers, has not been treated, and when one day the dog feels seriously threatened, he will bite without warning.

Understanding is the key to effective cures for problem behaviors. Punishment may seem like an effective way out, but it rarely is. If you are having problems with your puppy's behavior, try to think of things from his point of view. This will often lead you to a much better solution than one that merely makes life easier for you. We need to use our intelligence to solve problems, rather than resorting to aggression in an effort to try to force our dogs to behave.

Many dogs are punished for not understanding what their owners want them to do. Training is a long process, and few owners take the time and trouble needed to produce a well-trained dog. Many people do not understand that it takes many repetitions of the exercise for dogs to learn commands, and they expect too much of them as a result. Punishment will not help a dog to learn more quickly. It will simply learn to be afraid of the person administering the punishment. Because dogs are often confused about why they have received the punishment in the first place, they become wary of humans, expecting them to become angry and aggressive at any time.

What to do if Your Dog Has Problems

If, as your puppy matures, he develops behavior problems that you cannot understand or deal with, seek help from a person who has been specially trained to deal with such problems. Your vet should be able to recommend a dog behaviorist or a dog behavior counselor to you. Alternatively, write to one of the addresses on page 190.

Do not despair if things go wrong. Owners frequently have difficulties with their dogs' behavior, especially in the early years, and it is no disgrace to admit it. Despite the saying "you can't teach an old dog new tricks," it *is* possible, and even adult dogs with severe behavior problems can be changed, given the right treatment.

CHAPTER NINETEEN

ADOLESCENCE AND BEYOND

A very young puppy will be dependent on you for all his needs. Since you will be the center of his world, he will follow you around and be very willing to please. As he grows up, however, the focus of his world will shift to include the rest of his environment and he will begin to develop a more independent attitude. This process will begin when he is about 18 weeks old and builds up gradually until true adolescence is reached at about 6 months.

The change in your puppy's attitude at this time can be disheartening unless you know what to expect. At first you are in total control of your puppy, and he will be easy to teach and constantly attentive. Gradually, as he begins to mature and becomes more interested in what is going on around him, it will feel as though you are losing the closeness with him that you once enjoyed. He will be less easy to control and less willing to listen to what you want. Adolescence is a very selfish time, and what *he* wants will become more important than what you want.

At some point in your puppy's development, you will probably find that all the things he has learned seem to have been forgotten. Try not to worry about this too much, since they will not have been forgotten but put aside for the time being while he concentrates on other things. Persevere with your training, patiently insisting that he does exactly what you require.

It is tempting to get angry sometimes, but try to remember it is just a phase he is going through. Adolescent puppies can be exasperating and can lead to you becoming really angry and aggressive. Try to end a training session before you have reached this stage. If you feel yourself getting cross, ask your puppy to do something easy, such as "sit." Then praise him for doing this and end the session. Punishing your puppy will not help, but will only serve to put more distance between you both and make the rest of his environment seem even more attractive.

A common problem at this time is that of a dog does not come back when called during a walk. Since other things in the outside world now hold more interest your puppy may prefer to investigate rather than come back to you, no matter what rewards you are offering.

If this is beginning to happen, attach a long line to his collar before letting him run free. Call him back whenever he is getting to the end of

Adolescent puppies can be exasperating because they seem to have forgotten all you have taught them (left). Other things in the outside world will now hold their interest, and you will need to teach them that they have to do as you ask.

Use a long line to teach your puppy that he has to respond to all your commands (below).

the line and use the line to enforce the command if necessary. In this way, you will prevent him from learning that the unwanted behavior (running off) brings rewards. You will also be teaching him that he has no choice but to go back to you if he hears you call.

At about six months of age, sexual maturity occurs, and all the associated hormonal changes will bring about changes in your puppy's behavior. Bitches will come into season for the first time, and dramatic changes in temperament can occur just before and throughout the season. Male dogs experience less visible changes even, though their hormone levels are fluctuating wildly, but the effect on their temperament can be just as dramatic. They will become interested in females around this time, will begin to mark their territory in earnest, and will also be attempting to find their hierarchy status with any male dogs they encounter on a regular basis.

As reproduction plays an important role in evolution, activities associated with this will be of prime importance to your puppy at this time. What *you* want will seem less important to him and, while you should not give him the chance to disobey you, you will need to prevent him from getting his own way all the time. But be sympathetic to the fact that it is natural for his attention to be distracted.

Just like children going through their teenage years, adolescent puppies can be difficult to live with. Not only are they becoming more interested in the world around them than in you, they are also beginning to assert themselves and test how far they can push you and the limits you have set for them.

Since everyone in the family will have already made it obvious during his early life that he is the lowest in the hierarchy, your puppy should not be able to climb too far up the ladder. Tighten your hierarchy rules if necessary and try not to issue commands that cannot be enforced should your puppy decide to ignore them.

Adolescence will pass more easily if you know about it, expect it, and do not worry too much about it. Luckily, it does not last as long in dogs as it does in children, and by the time your puppy is 12 to 18 months old, it will have passed. During the adolescent phase it will sometimes seem that, even after all your careful early work, you now have a puppy that is more trouble than he is worth. Do not despair! Your puppy will mature into a dog that will once again look to you for decisions, be willing to please, and provided that you have continued with the training, be under your control.

Young Adults

Gradually your puppy will grow out of adolescence and become a young adult. At this age, all your hard work will start to pay off and you will begin to reap the rewards. He will still be filling out physically and emotionally for some time, but the difficult days of adolescence will be over and you can afford to relax a little now. Socialization needs to continue throughout a dog's life to some degree, but this should happen naturally as you take your well-mannered dog out and about with you. Training may need a little reinforcement from time to time, but the commands you instilled early on will not be forgotten, especially if they are in constant use.

In the End — It Really Does Work!

Obedient and well-socialized dogs are happy in themselves and are a pleasure to be with.

After all your dedication in the early months, you will eventually have a dog that is well mannered, obedient, and willing to please. He can live as a member of the family and be taken anywhere, or be left at home, without misbehaving.

He will be well socialized with a happy, outgoing nature. He will know how to play with humans, both adults and children, and will mix easily with other dogs as well. Since you have not stifled his character by over-disciplining him, he is free to be himself without fear of being punished, and his true character will shine through.

Your pet will repay the time and trouble you took during his puppy-hood many times over throughout the years. He will be a friend to come home to, loved and admired by all who know him, and a dog you will be proud to own.

Appendix: Socialization Program

Put a check in the box for each encounter. Enter as many checks per box as possible.
(Take care not to overwhelm your puppy — take things at his pace.)

Age	6-7 wk.	7-8 wk.	8-9 wk.	9-10 wk.	10-11 wk.	11-12 wk.	3-6 mo.	6-10 mo.
Adults (men and women)								
Young adults								
Middle-aged adults								
Elderly people								
Disabled/infirm								
Loud, confident people								
Shy, timid people								
Delivery people								
Joggers								
People wearing uniforms								
People wearing hats								
People with beards								
People wearing glasses								
People wearing motorcycle helmets								
Children								
Babies								
Toddlers								
Juniors								
Teenagers								

Age	6-7 wk.	7-8 wk.	8-9 wk.	9-10 wk.	10-11 wk.	11-12 wk.	3-6 mo.	6-10 mo.
Other animals								
Dogs — adults								
Dogs — puppies								
Cats								
Small pets								
Ducks								
Livestock								
Horses								
Environments								
Friend's house								
Shopping mall								
Park								
Outside a school								
Outside a children's play area								
Country walks								
Riding in a car								
City walks								
Outdoor restaurant								
Slippery floor								
Party								
Veterinarian's office								
Grooming parlor (if necessary)								
Boarding kennels								
Other								
Bicycles								
Motorcycles								
Cars								
Buses								
Trucks								

Bibliography

Bashkim, Dibra, with Elizabeth Randolph. *Teach Your Dog to Behave: Simple Solutions to Over 300 Common Dog Behavior Problems from A to Z.* New York: Dutton, 1993.

Benjamin, Carol L. *Dog Training for Kids.* Rev. ed. New York: Howell Book House, 1988.

Condax, Kate Delano. *101 Training Tips for Your Dog.* New York: Dell Publishing, Inc.,1994

Cusick, William. *Canine Nutrition and Choosing the Best Food for Your Breed of Dog.* 1st ed. Aloha, OR: Adele Publications, Inc., 1991.

Eckstein, Warren, with Andrea Eckstein. *How to Get Your Dog to Do What You Want: A Loving Approach to Unleashing Your Dog's Astonishing Potential.* New York: Columbine, 1994.

Evans, Job M. *The Evans Guide for Housetraining Your Dog.* New York: Howell Book House, 1987.

Fenger, Diane and Arlene F. Steinle. *The Standard Book of Dog Grooming.* Rev. ed. Fairfax, VA: Delinger's Publishers, Ltd., 1983.

Fogle, Bruce. *Know Your Dog: An Owner's Guide to Dog Behavior.* New York: Dorling Kindersly, 1992.

Fox, Michael. *Superdog: Raising the Perfect Canine Companion.* New York: Howell Book House, 1990.

Hart, Benjamin L and Lynette A. *The Perfect Puppy: How to Choose Your Dog By Its Behavior.* New York: W.H. Freeman & Company, 1988.

Milani, Myrna M. *The Body Language and Emotion of Dogs: A Practical Guide to the Physical and Behavioral Displays Owners and Dogs Exchange and How to Use Them to Create a Lasting Bond.* New York: William Morrow & Co., Inc., 1986.

Monks of New Skete. *How to Be Your Dog's Best Friend: A Training Manual for Dog Owners.* Little, Brown & Company Ltd., 1978

Mordecai, Siegal, and Matthew Margoli. *I Just Got a Puppy: What Do I Do?* New York: Simon & Schuster, 1992.

Mugford, Roger. *Never Say No: The Complete Program for a Happier and More Cooperative Dog.* New York: G.P. Putnam's Sons, 1994.

Neville, Peter. *Do Dogs Need Shrinks?.* New York: Citadel Press, 1992.

Olson, Bijorn S. *The Family Guide to Training Your Dog.* New York: Sterling Publishing. Co., Inc., 1991.

Tucker, Michael. *Solving Your Dog Problems: A Practical Handbook for Owners and Trainers.* New York: Howell Book House, 1992

Volhard, Joachim, and Melissa Bartlett. *What All Good Dogs Should Know: The Sensible Way to Train.* New York: Howell Book House, 1991.

Weitzman, Nan, and Embery, Joan. *The Good Dog Book: The Responsible Owner's Guide to a Happy & Healthy Pet,* 1993.

Weston, David, and Ross, Ruth. *Dog Problems: The Gentle Modern Cure.* New York: Howell Book House, 1992.

Useful Addresses

American Kennel Club (AKC)
51 Madison Avenue
New York, NY 10010-1686
(212) 696-8200

American Veterinary Society of Animal Behavior (AVSB)
c/o Dr. Ilana Reisner
NYSCVM Cornell University
Animal Behavior Clinic
Ithaca, NY 14853-3844
(607) 253-3844

United Kennel Club (UKC)
100 E. Kilgore Road
Kalamazoo, MI 49001-5598
(616) 343-9020

INDEX